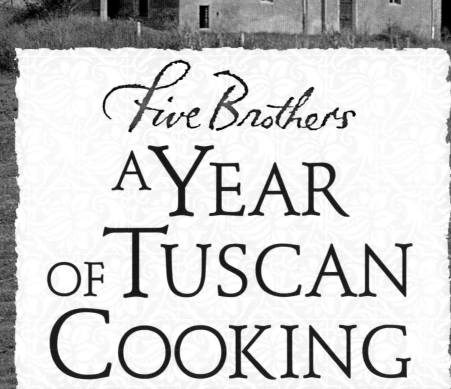

Five Brothers
A YEAR
OF TUSCAN
COOKING

FRIEDMAN/FAIRFAX
PUBLISHERS

A FRIEDMAN/FAIRFAX BOOK

Library of Congress Cataloging-in-Publication Data available upon request.

ISBN 1-56799-545-4

Recipe Development: Rosemary Smalberg
Text: Leah Rosch
Food Styling: Michael DiBeneditto
Prop Styling: Sylvia Lachter
Calligraphy: Bernard Maisner

Editor: Tony Burgess
Art Director: Jeff Batzli
Designer: Andrea Karman
Photography Director: Christopher C. Bain
Production Director: Karen Matsu Greenberg

Color separations by Colourscan Overseas Co Pte
Printed in Singapore by KHL Printing Co. Pte. Ltd.

For bulk purchases and special sales, please contact:
Friedman/Fairfax Publishers
Attention: Sales Department
15 West 26th Street
New York, New York 10010
212/685-6610   FAX 212/685-1307

Visit our website:
http://www.metrobooks.com

Contenuto
CONTENTS

FOREWORD

Twenty-five years ago, when I first opened Valentino, my restaurant in Los Angeles, I felt that I had an important mission to accomplish.

Arriving in the United States from my native Italy, I had been disappointed to find that, for many Americans, Italian cuisine meant little more than spaghetti and meatballs. I set out to introduce my customers to the authentic cuisine of Italy.

The genius of Italian cooking is that it allows the ingredients to speak for themselves, releasing and intermingling their flavors in simple and elegant combinations. For this reason, the freshness and quality of the ingredients is of absolutely vital importance. At Valentino I set down as a guiding principle that we would use only the best and very freshest ingredients in every dish we prepared. This was not always so easy; in those early days, some important ingredients could not be found in this country, while others were very hard to find at the level of quality that I required.

Much has changed since then, and we are now fortunate in that the quality and availability of authentic Italian ingredients in North America have improved greatly. It is now possible for anyone, with a little guidance, to prepare Italian food that is authentic and satisfying.

That's where this wonderful book comes in. *Five Brothers: A Year of Tuscan Cooking* is a beautiful and immensely useful guide to creating a wide variety of splendid dishes. All of the recipes in this book are true to the finest traditions of Tuscany, the heart of Italy and the home of that country's most celebrated cuisine. Besides exquisite recipes, this book is filled with useful tips and techniques that help to ensure success every time you cook. And the final chapter, "In the Tuscan Kitchen" (page 132—turn there first!), truly sets *A Year of Tuscan Cooking* apart from other cookbooks. With glossaries of Italian pastas, cheeses, herbs, and oils, as well as instructions for preparing and storing the essential elements of Tuscan cuisine, this chapter will tell you all you need to know to get started on a delicious voyage of discovery.

Welcome, and *buon appetito!*

—Piero Selvaggio

INTRODUCTION

THERE IS AN OLD SAYING IN ITALIAN: *"L'AMORE PER LA BUONA TAVOLA É AMORE PER LA VITA"*—"A PASSION FOR FOOD IS A PASSION FOR LIFE." THIS EXPRESSION COULD HAVE WELL DESCRIBED FIVE BROTHERS WHO, IT'S SAID, LIVED IN A SMALL VILLAGE IN TUSCANY AND SHARED A SPECIAL AFFINITY FOR FOOD. THEY KNEW HOW TO RAISE IT, HOW TO PREPARE IT, AND, MOST OF ALL, THEY KNEW HOW TO ENJOY IT. THESE FIVE BROTHERS ARE THE INSPIRATION FOR THIS COOKBOOK.

EACH ONE WAS SAID TO HAVE BROUGHT HIS OWN PARTICULAR TALENT TO THE MIX. THERE WAS VITTORIO, THE ELDEST, WHO KNEW INSTINCTIVELY THE MOST FRUITFUL TIMETABLES FOR PLANTING AND HARVESTING; RAPHAEL, WHO GREW THE MOST FLAVORFUL TOMATOES, WHICH, he would tell you, were not the largest, but those that were thin-skinned and heavy in your hand; Marcello, the middle brother, who, appropriately, was a master of balance—he knew, for example, the precise amount of parsley required to soften the sting of too much garlic in a dish, or how to mellow the tang of Parmesan with a touch of cream; Dante, the family "nose," could sense by smell alone which olive oil was at its most pure, when cheese was aged to its peak, and which basil would produce the tastiest pesto sauce; and Christophe, the youngest, who made a point of gathering herbs at dawn because he knew they were at their most aromatic before the sun burned off the morning dew.

It's fitting that the brothers hailed from Tuscany. A region situated in the middle of Italy, Tuscany comprises the splendid cities of Siena and Lucca, the coastal town of Livorno, and the majestic city of Florence, the Tuscan capital. Yet as a whole, the region is known as much for its pastoral countryside, dotted with some of the best olive groves and vineyards in the country, as for its food—uncomplicated, hearty fare made with only the freshest ingredients. This is also the principle behind the pasta sauces inspired by the five brothers, sauces you'll find used in inventive ways throughout this cookbook.

Tuscan cooking is often called *cucina rustica*—rustic, or peasant, cooking. Native Tuscans consider this characterization high praise because it reflects the old-world tradition of their cuisine—a classic, and classically unadulterated, style in which a handful of simple ingredients is transformed into a superbly satisfying and homey meal.

It would follow, then, that the kitchen is regarded as the heart of the home in Tuscany. But if the kitchen is the heart, the seasons are at the soul of Tuscan cooking—since selecting the finest, most flavorful ingredients should be done when they're at their peak. And in Italy, as here, each season provides a rich, ever-changing bounty with which to create wonderful, and wonderfully easy, dishes. This is why you'll find four chapters of this cookbook, each devoted to a different season—so that you may enjoy vegetables, greens, fruits, even seafood and meats at their freshest.

Of course, we're fortunate in this country to be able to get most produce year-round. What that means, within the context of this cookbook, is that if the ingredients are available, you can enjoy a distinctively spring dish in the fall or something reminiscent of summer during the frosty days of January. But beyond availability, the time of year also naturally influences the preparation of food, summoning a different kind of savoriness—for instance, meats and vegetables that you roast in winter are best suited to grilling in summer. The seasons even help determine, and enrich, traditional meals for holiday celebrations: spring lamb at Easter; squash, cranberries, and grapes for fall festivals; and root vegetables and meat-based dishes for winter holidays.

The recipes in this book are organized into complete menus, made up of the five courses of a traditional Italian meal. While each of these menus has been assembled with care to provide a balance of flavors, textures, and colors, you should feel free to mix and match courses to create your own menus. The courses, in their customary order, are: *antipasto*—the appetizer portion, composed of dishes that can be served hot or cold, often requiring little or no cooking; *primo piatto*—a first course, consisting of pasta, gnocchi, risotto, polenta or soup (which explains why native Italians never eat pasta and soup at the same meal); *secondo piatto*—the most elaborate portion, featuring meat, poultry or seafood; *contorno*—vegetable dishes or salads that literally add the "contours" of the meal; and *dolce*—dessert, which, in Tuscan cuisine, almost always revolves around fruit, often accented with nuts, but never fussy or labor-intensive. (In fact, the *dolce* can be as simple as a platter of fruit and cheese.)

Understandably, you may not always want to create four- and five-course affairs—but even Italians don't dine on full-scale meals every day. The real joy of Tuscan cooking is having the freedom to personalize a meal; from satisfying a simple craving with three, or even two, courses to pulling out all the stops and celebrating in rare form. The sole requirement: a

passionate appreciation of food at its best. And now that entertaining at home is enjoying a welcome resurgence here in our country, we hope you'll find the simple pleasures of *cucina toscana* the perfect complement to your own signature hosting style.

Buon Appetito!

Primavera

SPRING

THE PERENNIAL NEW BEGINNING, SPRING IS THE ONE SEASON THAT CAN NEVER COME FAST ENOUGH—BOTH HERE AND IN TUSCANY. SPRING IS OUR PSYCHIC REWARD FOR HAVING SURVIVED NATURE'S HIBERNATION. THE DAYS GROW LIGHTER, THE WEATHER KINDER, AS SUNSHINE CONSPIRES WITH RAIN SHOWERS TO COAX OUT OF THEIR LONG SLEEP THE FIRST CROP OF TENDER VEGETABLES—MOST NOTABLY, ASPARAGUS, ARTICHOKES, BROCCOLI RABE, SPINACH, AND SWEET GREEN ONIONS. IN FACT, MORE THAN RELYING ON THE CALENDAR OR WARMING TRENDS, ITALIANS TRUST THOSE FIRST ASPARAGUS SIGHTINGS AS REAL PROOF THAT SPRING HAS ARRIVED. SALAD LEAVES, PARTICULARLY ARUGULA AND DANDELION GREENS, ARE ALSO FLAVORFUL HARBINGERS OF THE SEASON, FOLLOWED LATER BY THE FIRST BLUSH OF STRAWBERRIES.

This is why in Tuscany spring is nowhere more welcome than in *LA CUCINA*, the kitchen. Because it's there that nature's new harvest provides the fresh and flavorful ingredients for which Tuscan cooking is famous. The menus and recipes that follow take their inspiration from the venerable traditions of Tuscany's springtime cuisine. Yet, with their emphasis on fresh produce and simple, elegant preparations, these recipes fit perfectly with today's pared-down cooking and entertaining styles.

And if springtime in Tuscany is marked by the lush transformation of landscapes, the season is also greeted with a generous, and contagious, spirit of hospitality. There, as here, it's suddenly easier to host spontaneous get-togethers—everyone, it seems, is more than ready to trade cabin fever for spring fever. So, consider inviting friends over for an informal Sunday night supper or a special, leisurely brunch. Or host a fancy dinner for the extended family and close friends; the Tuscan-inspired Neoclassic Dinner Party you'll find in this chapter is a gourmet delight, certain to satisfy sophisticated palates. Whatever your pleasure, take advantage of spring's vegetables at their peak. One thing's for sure: they'll be gone again before you know it.

Colazione di benvenuto alla primavera

Salutations of Spring Brunch (Serves 4)

This light, meatless menu combines ease and elegance in equal parts. The asparagus frittata (an Italian omelette) is quintessential spring. Choosing between the two pasta dishes will be no mean feat—they're both scrumptious. And in conclusion, one of Italy's favorite springtime desserts: nothing could be simpler and more palate-pleasing.

ASPARAGUS FRITTATA

LINGUINE WITH SPRING VEGETABLES

OR

PENNE PUTTANESCA

MIXED GREEN SALAD

STRAWBERRIES IN BALSAMIC VINEGAR

Frittata di asparagi

ASPARAGUS FRITTATA

Serve hot right from the skillet or at room temperature, sliced into wedges or bite-sized squares—versatility only adds to this dish's appeal.

½ POUND FRESH ASPARAGUS, CUT INTO 1-INCH PIECES

1 SMALL ONION, CHOPPED

1 TABLESPOON OLIVE OIL

6 EGGS, BEATEN

SALT AND FRESHLY GROUND BLACK PEPPER TO TASTE

½ CUP GRATED PARMESAN CHEESE, DIVIDED

Preheat broiler.

In a medium saucepan, blanch asparagus in boiling water for about 2 minutes, or until tender. Drain and rinse under cold water; set aside.

In a large non-stick skillet, sauté onion in olive oil until tender.

Season eggs with salt and pepper; stir in half the Parmesan. Pour egg mixture into heated skillet along with asparagus. Cook over medium heat until egg mixture sets, about 12 to 15 minutes. Do not stir. Top mixture with remaining Parmesan and place in broiler until light and puffy, about 5 minutes. Serves 4-6.

LINGUINE WITH SPRING VEGETABLES

Sweet peas and spinach add a fresh twist (and taste) to this light, quick-fix course. To make it a rustic supper staple, substitute pappardelle for the linguine.

3 CUPS GRILLED SUMMER VEGETABLE SAUCE
(SEE RECIPE, P. 136)

1 POUND LINGUINE, UNCOOKED

½ POUND SUGAR SNAP PEAS, STEMS REMOVED

4 CUPS FRESH SPINACH, RINSED WELL WITH STEMS REMOVED

SHREDDED PARMESAN CHEESE

In a medium saucepan, simmer sauce over low heat until heated through, stirring occasionally. Meanwhile, cook pasta according to package directions; during last 2 minutes of cooking, add sugar snap peas and spinach to pasta cooking water. Drain pasta and vegetables well. Spoon sauce over pasta and vegetables; sprinkle with Parmesan. Serves 4-6.

PENNE PUTTANESCA

This gutsy classic—named for the brothels where its fast preparation made it
the perfect repast between clients—is an olive lover's ambrosia.

2 CLOVES GARLIC, MINCED

3 TABLESPOONS OLIVE OIL

3 CUPS FRESH TOMATO BASIL SAUCE
(SEE RECIPE, P. 136)

½ CUP OIL-CURED OLIVES, PITTED AND CHOPPED

2 TABLESPOONS SMALL CAPERS, DRAINED

4 ANCHOVY FILETS, DRAINED AND CHOPPED

CRUSHED RED PEPPER FLAKES TO TASTE

½ TEASPOON OREGANO

SALT AND FRESHLY GROUND BLACK PEPPER TO TASTE

1 POUND PENNE, UNCOOKED

2 TABLESPOONS CHOPPED FRESH FLAT-LEAF ITALIAN PARSLEY

In a large skillet, lightly sauté garlic in olive oil over low heat. Add sauce, olives, capers, anchovies, crushed red pepper, oregano, salt, and pepper. Simmer over low heat about 15 minutes, stirring occasionally. While the sauce is simmering, cook penne according to package directions; drain well. Add flat-leaf Italian parsley to sauce just before serving. Spoon sauce over pasta. Serves 4-6.

MIXED GREEN SALAD

The olive vinaigrette zestily dresses these exotic lettuces. Topping with creamy Gorgonzola provides an extra little kick.

2 CLOVES GARLIC, CRUSHED

8 CUPS MIXED SALAD GREENS (ROMAINE, ARUGULA, RADICCHIO, ESCAROLE, MESCLUN)

Olive Vinaigrette:

¼ CUP EXTRA-VIRGIN OLIVE OIL

1 TABLESPOON BALSAMIC VINEGAR

½ TEASPOON SALT

FRESHLY GROUND BLACK PEPPER

½ TEASPOON BLACK OLIVE PASTE

CRUMBLED GORGONZOLA CHEESE

Rub inside of wooden salad bowl with crushed garlic. Add assorted mixed salad greens. Chill while making vinaigrette.

In a small bowl, whisk together olive oil, balsamic vinegar, salt, pepper and olive paste. Spoon dressing over chilled greens; toss lightly to coat. Serve with crumbled Gorgonzola. Serves 4-6.

Fragole all'aceto balsamico

STRAWBERRIES IN BALSAMIC VINEGAR

The vinegar's tartness actually brightens the fruit's flavor, and once chilled, the vinegar loses its bite. Rinse berries before hulling so they'll absorb less water.

1 QUART FRESH RIPE STRAWBERRIES, STEMS REMOVED

2 TABLESPOONS SUGAR

2 TABLESPOONS BALSAMIC VINEGAR

FRESH MINT LEAVES FOR GARNISH

Cut strawberries in half lengthwise. Place in a bowl and toss with sugar and vinegar. Chill at least 30 minutes. Toss just before serving. Spoon into shallow dessert bowls. Garnish with mint leaves. Serves 4-6.

Grande cena neoclassica

Neoclassic Dinner Party (Serves 6)

Here's a menu that all but guarantees a great evening. This risotto is a sophisticated crowd-pleaser (and well worth the effort). The asparagus vinaigrette—one of the season's special joys—adds a lovely splash of color. But if the mood calls for something more inspired, serve the broccoli rabe dish instead. It's authentic Tuscan at its most savory.

HOT ARTICHOKE CRAB DIP

TUSCAN TOMATO MUSHROOM RISOTTO

HERB-ROASTED CHICKEN

ASPARAGUS VINAIGRETTE

OR

SAUSAGE WITH BROCCOLI RABE

GELATO WITH STRAWBERRY SAUCE

Intingolo caldo di granchi al carciofo

HOT ARTICHOKE CRAB DIP

This deceptively simple antipasto is quite a rustic showpiece. Have it ready and waiting when guests arrive, and you won't have to worry about making small talk.

2 CLOVES GARLIC, MINCED

1 TABLESPOON OLIVE OIL

1 CAN (6 OZ.) SNOW CRABMEAT, DRAINED

2 CUPS CREAMY ALFREDO SAUCE (SEE RECIPE, P. 138)

3 TABLESPOONS SHERRY

1 CAN (14 OZ.) ARTICHOKE HEARTS, DRAINED AND FINELY CHOPPED

3 TABLESPOONS CHOPPED FRESH FLAT-LEAF ITALIAN PARSLEY

½ TEASPOON FINELY GRATED FRESH LEMON ZEST

PINCH CRUSHED RED PEPPER FLAKES (OPTIONAL)

1 ROUND LOAF CRUSTY TUSCAN PEASANT BREAD, HOLLOWED OUT

In a medium saucepan, lightly sauté garlic in olive oil. Add crabmeat, Alfredo sauce, sherry, and artichoke hearts. Simmer over low heat about 5 minutes or until heated through, stirring occasionally. Add parsley, lemon zest, and red pepper flakes just before serving. Spoon into hollowed-out loaf of Tuscan bread and serve hot as a dip with crostini or crackers. Makes about 3 cups.

Risotto toscano al pomodoro e funghi

TUSCAN TOMATO MUSHROOM RISOTTO

By its very nature, risotto is distinctive. And this richly hued, robust version
does the Italian rice specialty proud.

4 CUPS BEEF BROTH

2 CUPS MUSHROOM AND GARLIC GRILL SAUCE
(SEE RECIPE, P. 137)

2 CUPS ARBORIO RICE

1 TABLESPOON SWEET BUTTER

¼ CUP GRATED PARMESAN CHEESE

½ CUP CHOPPED FRESH FLAT-LEAF ITALIAN PARSLEY

OLIVE OIL INFUSED WITH TRUFFLES

In a saucepan, bring broth and sauce to a boil; reduce heat and
simmer. In a large saucepan, lightly sauté rice in butter, stirring
frequently. Add about 1½ cups heated sauce mixture to rice.
Continue to cook rice over low to medium heat, stirring fre-
quently. (Rice and liquid should maintain a low simmer.)
Continue adding heated sauce mixture gradually. Stir and
cook about 25 to 30 minutes or until rice is tender. Stir
Parmesan into risotto. Rice should be moist and creamy.
Garnish with parsley and drizzle lightly with truffle oil.
Serves 6.

The Three Rules to Perfect Risotto

**Rule #1: Patience. Risotto is a dish that can't be
rushed (but is well worth the perseverance).**

**Rule #2: After adding the initial quantity of stock
or other liquid, wait until all the liquid has been
absorbed while stirring before adding more—and
then, add only a ladleful at a time.**

**Rule #3: Stir, stir, stir. And don't stop until a taste
test reveals the rice tender but firm (figure on a
good 25 minutes). Successfully done risotto has
a creamy, porridge-like consistency.**

Pollo arrosto alle erbe

HERB-ROASTED CHICKEN

The combination of aromatic herbs and this creamy sherry sauce infuses the chicken with a nice, piquant flavor.

1 ROASTING CHICKEN (7 TO 8 POUNDS)

4 CLOVES GARLIC, MINCED

SALT AND FRESHLY GROUND BLACK PEPPER TO TASTE

¼ CUP OLIVE OIL, DIVIDED

1 CUP CHOPPED FRESH FLAT-LEAF ITALIAN PARSLEY

2 TABLESPOONS CHOPPED FRESH SAGE OR THYME

1 CUP CHICKEN BROTH, HOMEMADE OR CANNED

¼ CUP FRESH LEMON JUICE

PARSLEY FOR GARNISH

Sherry Alfredo Sauce

2 CUPS CREAMY ALFREDO SAUCE (SEE RECIPE, P. 138)

¾ OUNCE DRIED PORCINI MUSHROOMS

¼ CUP SHERRY

¼ TEASPOON WORCESTERSHIRE SAUCE

Preheat oven to 375° F.

Rub the inside of the chicken with about ½ teaspoon minced garlic; sprinkle with salt and pepper. Rub 2 tablespoons of the olive oil inside the cavity. Stuff the chicken with the remaining garlic, parsley, and sage. Place chicken in a roasting pan. Pour the chicken broth, lemon juice, and remaining olive oil over chicken. Bake 20 minutes per pound (about 2½ hours), basting frequently, until chicken is thoroughly cooked. When chicken is nearly done, prepare Sherry Alfredo Sauce. Carve chicken and arrange on a serving platter. Garnish with parsley. Serve with the sauce. Serves 6.

Sherry Alfredo Sauce

In a small saucepan, combine porcini and ¾ cup water; heat to boiling. Remove from heat; let stand, covered, 15 minutes. Drain through a fine sieve or doubled cheesecloth; reserve ¼ cup liquid and set aside. Rinse mushrooms of any grit; coarsely chop. In a saucepan, combine other ingredients with mushrooms and mushroom liquid. Simmer over medium heat until slightly reduced.

Asparagi vinaigrette

ASPARAGUS VINAIGRETTE

For something so sophisticated in flavor, it couldn't be simpler to make. For added ease,
prepare both asparagus and dressing a day in advance and refrigerate separately.

2 POUNDS FRESH ASPARAGUS, TOUGH ENDS REMOVED

8 ROMAINE LETTUCE LEAVES

3 TABLESPOONS RED WINE VINEGAR

¼ TEASPOON SALT

¼ TEASPOON SUGAR

¼ TEASPOON FRESHLY GROUND BLACK PEPPER

½ CUP EXTRA-VIRGIN OLIVE OIL

2 TABLESPOONS MINCED FRESH FLAT-LEAF ITALIAN PARSLEY

1 TABLESPOON MINCED FRESH BASIL

Peel asparagus stalks a few inches from the ends, leaving the tips intact. In a large skillet, cook asparagus in boiling salted water about 6 minutes or until tender. Rinse with cold water and drain. Arrange lettuce leaves on a serving platter. Place asparagus spears over lettuce; refrigerate. In a small bowl, combine vinegar, salt, sugar, pepper, olive oil, parsley and basil; whisk until thoroughly blended. Pour dressing over asparagus just before serving. Serves 6.

The Care and Choosing of Asparagus

Choosing the best-tasting asparagus is not for the colorblind. Asparagus is at its most tender when stalks are apple green and tips are purple-tinged. *Look for firm stalks with moist, tightly closed tips. *To prepare for cooking, snap off spears at the point where they break naturally (usually about one-quarter up from the end). *Asparagus is best cooked the same day of purchase. But spears can keep in the refrigerator for up to four days. *For maximum shelf life, you have two options: Wrap the ends in a damp paper towel and store spears tightly wrapped in a plastic bag in the refrigerator. Or, trim the very bottom of the stems, place spears upright in a pitcher one-quarter filled with water, and refrigerate.

Salsiccia e rapini

SAUSAGE WITH BROCCOLI RABE

The sausage's delicate sweetness tames this pungent springtime green. For a hearty first
course, braise the two longer in a little olive oil and serve atop pasta.

1 POUND SWEET ITALIAN SAUSAGE, CASINGS REMOVED

3 CLOVES GARLIC, MINCED

4 CUPS COARSELY CHOPPED BROCCOLI RABE, STEMS REMOVED

EXTRA-VIRGIN OLIVE OIL

In a large skillet, thoroughly cook sausage, crumbling with a
fork. Drain fat. Add garlic, continue to cook briefly.
Meanwhile, cook broccoli rabe in boiling water about 3 to 4
minutes; drain thoroughly. Add broccoli rabe to sausage; sauté
briefly. Drizzle with olive oil before serving. Serves 6.

Demystifying Broccoli Rabe

A staple of Italian cooking, this leafy green—it looks like
skinny broccoli shoots with lots of leaves and a few small,
broccoli-like buds—is actually a member of the turnip
family. Broccoli rabe has a pungent, almost bitter flavor,
but is a worthwhile acquired taste.

• Select shoots with thin stems, deep green leaves, and few
to no yellow flowers.

• To trim, remove any wilted or yellow leaves, yellow
flowers, and thick, tough stems. Cook up all the rest as is.

• For maximum shelf life (usually up to five days), wrap
in a plastic bag and refrigerate.

Gelato con salsa di fragole

GELATO WITH STRAWBERRY SAUCE

An ice cream sundae for grownups! For the most sophisticated taste, be sure the vermouth is Italian.

1 PINT FRESH RIPE STRAWBERRIES, HULLED

5 TABLESPOONS CONFECTIONERS' SUGAR

2 TABLESPOONS DRY WHITE ITALIAN VERMOUTH

1 TEASPOON FINELY GRATED LEMON ZEST

1 QUART VANILLA GELATO (OR PREMIUM ICE CREAM)

STRAWBERRIES FOR GARNISH

Place strawberries, sugar, and vermouth in a food processor bowl. Pureé until smooth. Stir in lemon zest. Refrigerate until ready to serve. Scoop gelato or ice cream into dessert dishes; top with strawberry sauce. Garnish with strawberries. Serves 6.

Cena rustica domenicale

Rustic Sunday Supper (Serves 6)

Want to feed the family's spring fever in palatable style? This menu is the cure. Starting with a full-flavored focaccia, Tuscany's favorite flat bread, there are two hearty pasta options; a tangy and colorful salad; and for dessert, the lightest and crispest almond cookies. Here's one meal sure to keep the family around the supper table.

FOCACCIA WITH ARUGULA AND SUN-DRIED TOMATOES

SPINACH CANNELLONI

OR

PENNE WITH TOMATO CREAM SAUCE

MIXED GREENS WITH ORANGES AND RED ONION SALAD

ALMOND MACAROON CRISPS

Focaccia alla rucola e pomodori secchi

FOCACCIA WITH ARUGULA AND SUN-DRIED TOMATOES

Cooking mellows the slightly bitter taste of arugula, a key flavor component in this zesty, seasonal variation on basic focaccia.

1 Basic Focaccia, halved (see recipe, p. 33)

½ cup Creamy Alfredo Sauce (see recipe, p. 138)

2 tablespoons chopped sun-dried tomatoes

4 ounces fresh mozzarella cheese, drained and sliced

2 cloves garlic, slivered

1 cup fresh arugula leaves, coarsely chopped

Preheat oven to 425°F.

Prepare and bake focaccia as directed.

Spoon sauce over focaccia. Sprinkle with sun-dried tomatoes. Top with mozzarella slices, garlic and arugula. Bake 8-10 minutes or until bubbly. Cut into squares to serve. Serves 6.

Focaccia semplice
BASIC FOCACCIA

5 CUPS UNBLEACHED ALL-PURPOSE FLOUR

2 TEASPOONS SALT

2 CUPS WARM WATER (105°-115° F)

1 PACKAGE ACTIVE DRY YEAST

3 TABLESPOONS EXTRA-VIRGIN OLIVE OIL

ADDITIONAL OLIVE OIL FOR DRIZZLING

In a large bowl, combine flour and salt; set aside. In another bowl, combine warm water with yeast; stir. Let stand until yeast has dissolved, about 5 minutes. Whisk in olive oil. Add yeast mixture to flour. Using an electric mixer, mix on low speed about 2 minutes or until well combined. Remove dough from bowl; place on a lightly floured surface and knead until a smooth ball of dough forms. Place dough in bowl; cover and let rise 1 to 1½ hours or until doubled. Generously oil a 17 × 13-inch baking sheet. Place dough in pan; press and stretch dough evenly with oiled fingers to fill pan. Pierce dough with a fork at 1-inch intervals; drizzle lightly with olive oil. Cover dough with a kitchen towel and let rise about 45 minutes or until doubled.

Preheat oven to 450° F.

Bake about 20 minutes or until golden brown. Place on a rack to cool. Serve as is or top with herbs and other flavorings.

The Story on Focaccia

The precursor to our modern pizza, this large, flat, rectangular or round bread has actually been around for centuries. The word itself is Latin and means "from the floor of the fireplace"—referring to the literal preparation employed by the Etruscans, who baked flat dough on the stones of the kitchen hearth. Though it never went out of style in Tuscany, focaccia has been enjoying a trendy existence here recently among restaurant chefs and recreational cooks alike—perhaps because the bread is so versatile. Pre- or post-baking, the dough can be topped, stuffed or seasoned with just about any palate-pleasing ingredient imaginable. Once baked, it can then be eaten as is—for an antipasto or snack—or sliced in half for the flavorful foundation of a *panino*, an Italian-style sandwich. In its purest and, many say, most satisfying form, focaccia is drizzled with olive oil and sprinkled with salt before baking—certifying that sometimes there's no need to improve on simplicity.

Cannelloni alla fiorentina

SPINACH CANNELLONI

The trick to this updated Italian classic is the cheese. Select only the most full-bodied and you'll have an easy family favorite on your hands.

1¼ POUNDS FRESH SPINACH, THOROUGHLY RINSED WITH STEMS REMOVED (OR 1 PACKAGE [10 OZ.] FROZEN CHOPPED SPINACH, THAWED AND SQUEEZED DRY)

2 POUNDS PART-SKIM RICOTTA CHEESE

1 PACKAGE (8 OZ.) SHREDDED ITALIAN CHEESE BLEND (FONTINA, ROMANO, PARMESAN, MOZZARELLA, ASIAGO)

½ CUP GRATED PARMESAN CHEESE, DIVIDED

3 EGGS

SALT AND FRESHLY GROUND BLACK PEPPER TO TASTE

1 TABLESPOON CHOPPED FRESH FLAT-LEAF ITALIAN PARSLEY

1 TEASPOON DRIED BASIL

3 CUPS FRESH TOMATO BASIL SAUCE (SEE RECIPE, P. 136)

½ PACKAGE (16 OZ.) LASAGNA NOODLES, COOKED, DRAINED, AND CUT IN HALF CROSSWISE

1 CUP CREAMY ALFREDO SAUCE (SEE RECIPE, P. 138)

Preheat oven to 375°F.

In a large bowl, thoroughly combine spinach, ricotta and Italian cheeses, ¼ cup Parmesan, eggs, salt, pepper, parsley, and basil. Pour 1½ cups Fresh Tomato Basil sauce evenly in a 13 × 9-inch baking dish. Evenly spoon about ⅓ cup spinach-cheese filling in the center of each lasagna noodle half. Roll ends around filling; place seam-side down in prepared baking dish. Repeat, making 18. Top each with a dollop of Alfredo sauce. Evenly sprinkle with remaining Parmesan. Bake, covered, 1 hour. Uncover, bake 10 minutes or until bubbly. Let stand 5 minutes before serving. Serves 6-8.

Penne alla rosé

PENNE WITH TOMATO CREAM SAUCE

Subtle flavorings, substantial pasta, and simple preparation make this the perfect
choice for a casual supper anytime.

2 CUPS FRESH TOMATO BASIL SAUCE (SEE RECIPE, P.136)

¾ CUP LIGHT CREAM

1 POUND PENNE, COOKED AND DRAINED

SHAVED PARMESAN CHEESE FOR GARNISH

In a medium saucepan, thoroughly heat sauce. Add cream; stir to mix well and remove from heat. Serve over hot penne. Garnish with shaved Parmesan. Serves 4-6.

Insalata verde con arance e cipolle rosse

MIXED GREENS WITH ORANGES AND RED ONION SALAD

**Both delicious and decorative, this aromatic salad is a palate-pleasing foil to rich,
cheesy pasta dishes.**

7 CUPS ARUGULA OR ASSORTED MIXED GREENS,
RINSED AND TRIMMED

2 MEDIUM ORANGES, PEELED AND WHITE PITH REMOVED,
CUT INTO SECTIONS

1 SMALL RED ONION, THINLY SLICED

¼ CUP EXTRA-VIRGIN OLIVE OIL

2 TABLESPOONS FRESH LEMON JUICE

SALT AND FRESHLY GROUND BLACK PEPPER TO TASTE

In a large salad bowl, combine greens, orange sections and onion. Mix olive oil and lemon juice, drizzle over salad. Season with salt and pepper. Toss to coat well. Serves 4-6.

ALMOND MACAROON CRISPS

These light confections will have you parting with store-bought amaretti cookies for good. For tasteful authenticity, serve with espresso.

¾ CUP BLANCHED ALMONDS, VERY FINELY GROUND

¾ CUP SUGAR

2 LARGE EGG WHITES, AT ROOM TEMPERATURE

¼ TEASPOON ALMOND EXTRACT

Preheat oven to 350°F.

Line 3 baking sheets with parchment paper or aluminum foil; set aside. In a large bowl, combine almonds and sugar; stir to mix well. In another bowl, whisk together egg whites and almond extract until soft peaks form. Add egg whites to the almond mixture. Stir to form a soft batter. With a teaspoon, spoon batter onto baking sheets, spacing cookies apart, about 12 cookies per sheet. Bake in center of oven about 15 minutes or until lightly browned. Remove from oven and transfer parchment paper to cooling racks until cookies begin to firm up, about 3 to 4 minutes. With a sharp knife, lift cookies from parchment and transfer to racks to cool completely. Makes about 36 cookies.

Estate

SUMMER

SUMMER TRANSLATES TO EASY COOKING AND ENTERTAINING—NO MAT-TER WHICH SIDE OF THE ATLANTIC YOU'RE ON. FORTUNATELY, THE MANY DISTINCTIVE FLAVORS OF THE SEASON PROVIDE MOST ALL THE INGREDI-ENTS FOR CREATING TEMPTING TUSCAN DISHES. CONSIDER THE WIDE ARRAY OF VEGETABLES, FRUITS, AND HERBS IN SEASON: EGGPLANT, ESCA-ROLE, SUMMER SQUASH AND FAVA BEANS, FRESH TARRAGON AND PARSLEY, FIGS, PEACHES, PLUMS, AND SWEET-TART BERRIES. IN TUSCAN CUISINE, THESE ARE THE EPICUREAN EQUIVALENTS OF AN EMBARRASSMENT OF RICHES. SEAFOOD, TOO, IS AT ITS PEAK NOW. AND THEN THERE ARE SUMMER'S CROWN JEWELS: VINE-RIPENED, RED TOMATOES AND FRESH, AROMATIC BASIL—A COMBINATION THAT RESONATES *CUCINA ITALIANA* IN ITS EVERY REGIONAL VARIATION.

BUT JUST BECAUSE EASE AND SIMPLICITY REIGN DOESN'T MEAN SUMMER FOOD IS UNCEREMONIAL. THE CITY OF SIENA, FOR INSTANCE, SERVES UP EXQUISITE FARE OF CURED MEATS, FISH, AND HERB-SEASONED VEGETABLE DISHES TO ACCOMPANY THE CEREMONIES OF ITS CEN- TURIES-OLD *PALIO* FESTI- VAL, THE FAMED HORSE RACES HELD EVERY JULY 2ND AND AUGUST 16TH IN THE *PIAZZA DEL CAMPO*. AND THE SUMMER SOLSTICE GETS ITS DUE IN STARLIT SUPPERS SHARED ON PIAZZAS THROUGHOUT THE CITIES AND TOWNS OF TUSCANY. SURRENDERING TO THE LANGUID DAYS AND WARM, BREEZY EVENINGS, NATIVE ITALIANS HAVE MANAGED TO ELEVATE THE SEASON'S EATING TO AN ART FORM, SIMPLY BY MOVING MEALS FROM INDOORS OUT. AMONG THEIR FAVORITE PASTIMES, IT SEEMS, IS COOLING OFF IN THE SHADE OF A CAFÉ UMBRELLA WITH A *GRANITA*—A FROZEN DELICACY OF ICES, STRONG ESPRESSO (OR

FRUIT JUICE), AND SUGAR. (TO MAKE, COMBINE FOUR PARTS LIQUID TO ONE PART SUGAR; POUR INTO A STAIN- LESS-STEEL BAKING PAN. FREEZE FOR TWO HOURS, MASHING WITH A WHISK AT 15- TO 20-MINUTE INTER- VALS UNTIL MIXTURE HAS A GRAINY-SLUSHY TEXTURE. FREEZE FOR ANOTHER 15 MINUTES BEFORE SERVING IN INDIVIDUAL GLASSES.)

THESE DAYS, DINING *AL FRESCO* IS AS MUCH A PART OF OUR SUMMER VERNACU- LAR AS THEIRS. THIS IS WHY YOU'LL FIND TWO OF THE FOLLOWING THREE MENUS GEARED TO THE GREAT OUTDOORS; IN THE FORM OF A SHADY MEADOW (OR SEASIDE) PICNIC AND A SAVORY BACKYARD BAR- BEQUE—IN WHICH WE CELEBRATE THE CLASSIC TUSCAN-COOKING CHARACTERISTIC OF GRILLING PRACTICALLY EVERYTHING IN SIGHT. THE POINT TO REMEMBER: SAVOR THE FLAVORS OF SUMMER—THEY DON'T GET MUCH BETTER THAN THIS.

Picnic per un bel giorno di sole

Picnic for a Perfectly Cloudless Day (Serves 4 to 6)

This picnic offering is more like a moveable feast. The chilled soup will tastefully cool off a crowd. With a little advance prep, the three flavorful *panini*—sophisticated sandwiches with an Italian accent—can be ready to go in no time. And for dessert, two delectable treats...because summertime calls for a little indulgence. Load a cooler with ice, pack everything in—and have a great time.

CHILLED TOMATO SOUP

GRILLED CHICKEN WITH OLIVE PESTO ON PEASANT BREAD

WILD GREENS AND GORGONZOLA PANINI

TUNA AND MARINATED ARTICHOKE PANINI

DESSERT BRUSCHETTA WITH BERRIES

CHOCOLATE WALNUT BISCOTTI

Zuppa fredda di pomodoro

CHILLED TOMATO SOUP

A refreshing summer soup (think gazpacho with Italian herbs) whose ingredients work well in several forms: diced, coarsely chopped or pureed.

2 CUPS FRESH TOMATO BASIL SAUCE (SEE RECIPE, P. 136)

1 CUP FINELY CHOPPED CUCUMBER

½ CUP FINELY CHOPPED GREEN PEPPER

¼ CUP THINLY SLICED SCALLIONS

3 TABLESPOONS TARRAGON VINEGAR

3 CLOVES GARLIC, MINCED

2 TABLESPOONS OLIVE OIL

2 TABLESPOONS MINCED FRESH FLAT-LEAF ITALIAN PARSLEY

1 TABLESPOON MINCED FRESH CHIVES

1 TEASPOON WORCESTERSHIRE SAUCE

½ TEASPOON HOT PEPPER SAUCE

¼ TEASPOON FRESHLY GROUND BLACK PEPPER

3 CUPS TOMATO JUICE

In a large bowl, combine all ingredients. Cover and refrigerate at least 4 hours. Serve chilled. Serves 6.

Pollo alla griglia con salsa d'olive su pane rustico

GRILLED CHICKEN WITH OLIVE PESTO ON PEASANT BREAD

Save time and cook the chicken breasts in advance. The zesty olive pesto that dresses these panini can liven up even leftovers.

Marinade:

1 CLOVE GARLIC, MINCED

1 TABLESPOON EXTRA-VIRGIN OLIVE OIL

1 TABLESPOON BALSAMIC VINEGAR

2 BONELESS CHICKEN BREASTS (ABOUT ½ POUND)

Olive Pesto:

¼ CUP CHOPPED FRESH FLAT-LEAF ITALIAN PARSLEY

2 TABLESPOONS CHOPPED PITTED GREEN OLIVES

1 TABLESPOON CAPERS, DRAINED

1 CLOVE GARLIC

¼ TEASPOON FINELY GRATED LEMON ZEST

2 TABLESPOONS EXTRA-VIRGIN OLIVE OIL

1 TABLESPOON FRESH LEMON JUICE

SALT AND COARSELY GROUND BLACK PEPPER TO TASTE

4 SLICES TUSCAN PEASANT BREAD

In a shallow bowl or plastic bag, combine garlic, olive oil, and balsamic vinegar. Add chicken breasts; coat with marinade on all sides. Marinate in the refrigerator 2 to 3 hours.

While chicken is marinating, prepare olive pesto by combining parsley, olives, capers, garlic, lemon zest, olive oil, lemon juice, salt, and pepper in a food processor bowl. Process until mixture has a coarse texture. Set aside and chill until ready to serve.

Preheat grill. Remove chicken from marinade. Grill, turning several times until chicken is thoroughly cooked, about 15 to 20 minutes. Slice grilled chicken. Arrange on sliced bread. Spoon olive pesto over chicken. Top with second slice of bread; cut each in half. Makes 4 half sandwiches.

Panini alla Gorgonzola e all'insalata di campo

WILD GREENS AND GORGONZOLA PANINI

The pungent Gorgonzola has both a palatable and a practical use: It's the tasty glue
that holds these delicious sandwiches together.

4 SLICES CRUSTY TUSCAN PEASANT BREAD OR FOCACCIA

4 OUNCES GORGONZOLA CHEESE, AT ROOM TEMPERATURE

½ JAR (6 OZ.) ROASTED RED PEPPERS, DRAINED
AND SLICED IN STRIPS

4 ARUGULA LEAVES

2 ESCAROLE LEAVES, COARSELY CHOPPED

2 RADICCHIO LEAVES, SLICED

1 TABLESPOON EXTRA-VIRGIN OLIVE OIL

4 TEASPOONS BALSAMIC VINEGAR

SALT AND FRESHLY GROUND BLACK PEPPER TO TASTE

Spread bread slices with Gorgonzola. Evenly divide roasted
pepper strips over cheese. Top with greens and drizzle with
olive oil, balsamic vinegar and season with salt and pepper.
Top each *panino* with another bread slice and press down
lightly; cut each in half. Makes 4 half sandwiches.

An Appreciation of *Panini*

Literally speaking, *panini* means little breads. But
what the word really refers to are delectable Italian-
style sandwiches. And in a cuisine that respects bread
as much as Tuscan, the pairing of a roll or two chunky
slices of bread with a few fresh, flavorful ingredients is
a natural. The breads that make the best *panino*: *filone*,
cigar-shaped loaves; *michette*, which are round, hollow
rolls; and thick slices of *pane toscano*, chewy rustic
round loaves. But in a pinch, any crusty, quality bakery
bread will do.

Panini al tonno e ai carciofini marinati

TUNA AND MARINATED ARTICHOKE PANINI

**The rustic combination of tuna, artichokes, and black olives in these sandwiches is
wonderfully evocative of Tuscan fare.**

1 JAR (6 OZ.) MARINATED ARTICHOKE HEARTS, DRAINED

2 TABLESPOONS BLACK OLIVE SPREAD

2 CRUSTY LARGE ROLLS, CUT IN HALF HORIZONTALLY

1 CAN (6½ OZ.) IMPORTED TUNA IN OLIVE OIL, DRAINED

½ CUP ARUGULA

Slice artichoke hearts in half lengthwise, if large. Spread bottom halves of rolls with olive spread. Top with tuna, arugula, and artichoke hearts. Cover with the tops of the rolls; cut each in half. Makes 4 half sandwiches.

Bruschetta dolce ai lamponi

DESSERT BRUSCHETTA WITH BERRIES

**"Luscious" is the only word for this sweet treat. To transport, pack all the fixings
separately and assemble before serving.**

6 SLICES CRUSTY BREAD, ABOUT ½-INCH THICK

8 OUNCES MASCARPONE CHEESE, AT ROOM TEMPERATURE

2 TABLESPOONS HONEY OR BROWN SUGAR

1 PINT FRESH RASPBERRIES

Lightly grill or toast bread slices. While still warm, spread with mascarpone. Drizzle with honey (or sprinkle with brown sugar). Top with raspberries. Serves 6.

Biscotti di cioccolato alle noci

CHOCOLATE-WALNUT BISCOTTI

**The raves these superior Italian cookies garner—from adults and kids alike—
make them more than worth the little extra effort.**

2 CUPS CHOPPED WALNUTS

3 OUNCES UNSWEETENED CHOCOLATE

⅓ CUP UNSALTED BUTTER

2 CUPS FLOUR

2 TEASPOONS BAKING POWDER

3 LARGE EGGS

1 CUP SUGAR

2 TEASPOONS FINELY GRATED ORANGE ZEST

Preheat oven to 350°F.

Place walnuts on a cookie sheet; toast about 10 minutes or until golden brown.

In a double boiler over simmering water, melt chocolate and butter together. Remove from heat and stir until smooth. Let mixture cool.

In a bowl, sift together the flour and baking powder. In a large bowl, beat the eggs lightly. Gradually add sugar; beat until light and fluffy. Add orange zest. Stir in cooled chocolate mixture. Stir in the flour and baking powder until well blended. Add walnuts; stir to mix well. Divide dough in half, wrap in plastic wrap and chill at least 1 hour.

Preheat oven to 350°F. On a greased baking sheet, form into two flattened logs, each about 14 inches long × 2½ inches wide. Place 4 inches apart on baking sheet. Bake 40 minutes or until logs are firm when pressed in the center.

Remove from oven. On a cutting board, cut logs crosswise on the diagonal into ½-inch slices. Return to oven, arranging biscotti cut-side down on baking sheet. Bake 10-15 minutes or until crisp. Transfer to rack to cool. Store in airtight container. Makes about 3 dozen.

Cenetta al tramonto

Light Sunset Supper (Serves 4 to 6)

This lovely meal works equally well indoors or out. In addition to its several choices and wonderful array of flavors, it's easy on the cook. If you're starting with the roasted-eggplant crostini, serve the salad as your vegetable course. But for a true Tuscan summer taste sensation, opt for the special fava bean antipasto, and make the charred peppers and eggplant your vegetable side. Both pasta selections are smashing—and so simple that you practically can decide at the last minute which better suits the mood. To finish, a combo of the freshest fruit tastes of the season.

CROSTINI WITH SAVORY ROASTED EGGPLANT

OR

FAVA BEAN ANTIPASTO

RADIATORE PASTA SALAD

OR

FARFALLE WITH HERB-MARINATED GRILLED SHRIMP

MIXED GREENS WITH TOASTED WALNUTS AND PARMESAN

OR

CHARRED PEPPERS AND ROASTED EGGPLANT

FRESH FRUIT SALAD WITH GELATO

Crostini alle melanzane arrosto
CROSTINI WITH SAVORY ROASTED EGGPLANT

A roasted red pepper is the secret ingredient here, infusing the eggplant mixture with a hint of rustic, smoky flavor.

Eggplant Spread:

1 SMALL EGGPLANT, PEELED AND SLICED THICKLY

1 TABLESPOON OLIVE OIL

1 CLOVE GARLIC, MINCED

½ CUP MARINARA SAUCE WITH BURGUNDY WINE
(SEE RECIPE, P. 137)

¼ CUP CHOPPED ROASTED RED PEPPERS, HOMEMADE OR JARRED

1 TEASPOON SMALL CAPERS, DRAINED

SALT AND FRESHLY GROUND BLACK PEPPER TO TASTE

Preheat oven to 425° F.

Place eggplant slices on a lightly greased baking sheet. Combine olive oil and garlic; brush on both sides of eggplant. Bake 40 minutes, turning eggplant slices halfway through. Cool slightly. On a cutting board, coarsely chop eggplant. In a bowl, combine with sauce, roasted peppers, capers, salt and pepper; mix well.

Crostini:

½ BAGUETTE, CUT INTO ½-INCH SLICES (ABOUT 24)

EXTRA-VIRGIN OLIVE OIL

½ TEASPOON OREGANO, ROSEMARY, OR THYME

1 LARGE CLOVE GARLIC, CRUSHED

Preheat oven to 400° F.

Brush both sides of bread slices with olive oil and arrange on a baking sheet. Sprinkle with oregano, rosemary or thyme. Bake about 8 minutes or until lightly golden. Remove from oven, rub one side with crushed garlic. Top with roasted eggplant spread. Arrange on serving platter. Serve warm or at room temperature. Makes 24 crostini.

FAVA BEAN ANTIPASTO

Antipasto di fave

The appearance of fava beans is one of the first signs of summer in Tuscany. And the younger and more delicate the bean, the sweeter its taste.

3 POUNDS FRESH TENDER FAVA BEANS

4 OUNCES ROMANO OR PARMESAN CHEESE, DICED

3 TABLESPOONS EXTRA-VIRGIN OLIVE OIL

2 TABLESPOONS MINCED FRESH FLAT-LEAF ITALIAN PARSLEY

SALT AND FRESHLY GROUND BLACK PEPPER TO TASTE

CRUSTY TUSCAN BREAD

Remove beans from the pod and blanch about 20 seconds in boiling water. Drain and rinse with cold water. Peel outer covering from each bean. In a medium bowl, combine beans, cheese, olive oil, parsley, salt, and pepper. Marinate at least 1 hour in the refrigerator. Serve with crusty Tuscan bread. Serves 4-6.

Insalata fredda di radiatori

RADIATORE PASTA SALAD

**This is one of those perfect, all-purpose summer pasta recipes. Keep its uncomplicated
ingredients on hand—you never know when you'll want to whip it up.**

Dressing:

1 CUP MUSHROOM AND GARLIC GRILL SAUCE (SEE RECIPE,
P. 137)

3 TABLESPOONS EXTRA-VIRGIN OLIVE OIL

2 TABLESPOONS BALSAMIC VINEGAR

2 TABLESPOONS MINCED FRESH FLAT-LEAF ITALIAN PARSLEY

1 TABLESPOON MINCED FRESH BASIL

SALT AND FRESHLY GROUND BLACK PEPPER TO TASTE

1 PACKAGE (14 OZ.) RADIATORE PASTA, COOKED AND DRAINED

2 RED OR YELLOW BELL PEPPERS, DICED

2 CUPS FRESH BROCCOLI, STEAMED UNTIL TENDER AND DRAINED

¼ CUP OIL-CURED OLIVES, DRAINED AND SLICED

1 CUP DICED PROVOLONE OR MOZZARELLA CHEESE

2 TABLESPOONS CAPERS, DRAINED

In a small bowl, combine sauce, olive oil, balsamic vinegar,
parsley, basil, salt, and pepper; set aside.

In a large bowl, combine radiatore pasta, peppers, broccoli,
olives, cheese, and capers. Pour dressing over salad; toss to
coat well. Cover and chill until ready to serve. Serves 6.

Farfalle con gamberi alla griglia

FARFALLE WITH HERB-MARINATED GRILLED SHRIMP

**If you're in the mood for a little grilling, this light, piquant pasta dish is a
cinch—and pretty, too.**

1 POUND EXTRA-LARGE FRESH SHRIMP, PEELED AND DEVEINED

¼ CUP EXTRA-VIRGIN OLIVE OIL

2 TABLESPOONS BALSAMIC VINEGAR

1 TABLESPOON LEMON JUICE

1 TABLESPOON FINELY CHOPPED FRESH BASIL

1 TABLESPOON MINCED FRESH FLAT-LEAF ITALIAN PARSLEY

1 TEASPOON FINELY CHOPPED FRESH OREGANO

PINCH CRUSHED RED PEPPER FLAKES

1 POUND FARFALLE, COOKED AND DRAINED

3 CUPS MARINARA SAUCE WITH BURGUNDY WINE (SEE
RECIPE, P. 137), HEATED

PARSLEY SPRIGS FOR GARNISH

Butterfly raw shrimp, leaving tail on, if desired. Place shrimp
in a bowl; add olive oil, balsamic vinegar, lemon juice, basil,
parsley, oregano, and crushed red pepper flakes. Stir to coat
shrimp thoroughly. Marinate shrimp for at least 3 hours in the
refrigerator. Preheat grill. Remove shrimp from marinade.
Grill about 6 minutes or until shrimp are cooked, turning frequently.

Fill individual bowls with cooked farfalle. Spoon on heated
sauce and top with grilled shrimp. Garnish with parsley.
Serves 6.

Insalata verde con noci tostate e Parmigiano

MIXED GREENS WITH TOASTED WALNUTS AND PARMESAN

The walnuts and Parmesan add a welcome depth of flavor and texture to this already
charming salad of mixed exotic greens.

4 TABLESPOONS COARSELY CHOPPED WALNUTS

¼ CUP EXTRA-VIRGIN OLIVE OIL

2 TABLESPOONS BALSAMIC VINEGAR

SALT AND FRESHLY GROUND BLACK PEPPER TO TASTE

8 CUPS MIXED SALAD GREENS (ROMAINE, ARUGULA, ESCAROLE, RADICCHIO, MESCLUN)

SHAVED PARMESAN CHEESE

Preheat oven to 350° F.

Place walnuts on a baking sheet. Bake 8-10 minutes or until lightly toasted; set aside. Combine mixed greens in a large bowl; chill. In a small bowl, combine olive oil, balsamic vinegar, salt, and pepper. Pour dressing over chilled salad greens; toss lightly to coat. Serve salad on individual salad plates. Top with toasted walnuts and shaved Parmesan. Serves 4-6.

Peperoni alla brace e melanzane arrosto

CHARRED PEPPERS AND ROASTED EGGPLANT

Such a simple dish with such robust flavors. This recipe works equally well
for grilling the vegetables.

1 MEDIUM EGGPLANT, PEELED AND CUT INTO 1-INCH SLICES

1 TABLESPOON OLIVE OIL

SALT AND FRESHLY GROUND BLACK PEPPER TO TASTE

2 RED BELL PEPPERS, CHARRED

1 TEASPOON CHOPPED FRESH OREGANO OR THYME

Preheat oven to 400° F.

Arrange eggplant in a large roasting pan. Drizzle with olive
oil. Season with salt and pepper; toss to coat evenly. Bake
about 40 minutes. Add charred peppers; bake an additional 10
minutes or until vegetables are tender and edges begin to
brown. Stir frequently during baking. Transfer to serving dish.
Add fresh herbs just before serving. Serves 4-6.

Alternate Tricks to Roasting Red Peppers

Trick #1: With metal tongs, hold the pepper over the
flame of a gas stove or place directly on the heating element of an electric stove. Turn, till each side is lightly
charred and blistered. Place the pepper in a closed
paper bag to steam. When cool to the touch, gently
rub off skin by hand. Make sure to remove all traces of
blackened skin—but don't rinse under running water,
or you'll wash away flavor, as well.

Trick #2: Place peppers under a preheated oven broiler
or on a charcoal grill no more than 3 inches from the
heat source. Cook, turning till lightly charred and blistered on all sides. Transfer peppers to a bowl and cover
tightly. When cool, peel off skins by hand.

Macedonia di frutta fresca al gelato

FRESH FRUIT SALAD WITH GELATO

**The trick to this dish: combine as many varieties of fruit as possible. Allowing them
to co-mingle in this citrus-juice marinade only enhances their fresh flavors.**

2 POUNDS ASSORTED FRESH FRUIT (PEACHES, CHERRIES,
MELONS, FIGS, NECTARINES, PLUMS, BERRIES, APPLES, PEARS)

1 CUP ORANGE JUICE

GRATED PEEL OF ½ LEMON

JUICE OF 1 LEMON

¼ CUP SUGAR

1 QUART VANILLA GELATO (OR PREMIUM ICE CREAM)

Peel and slice fruit; place in a large bowl. Add remaining
ingredients; toss lightly to coat. Marinate 4 hours in the refrigerator. Serve with gelato. Serves 4–6.

Grigliata del solstizio d'estate

Summer Solstice Barbeque (Serves 10)

Tuscans are grill crazy—and once you taste these savory flavors, you'll understand why. Serve this menu to celebrate the summer solstice in June. Then bring it out again for your Labor Day *festa*. It's fitting to bid farewell to summer in the same manner in which you ushered it in. Besides, for a real celebration, hot dogs and hamburgers can't hold a candle to this fare.

GRILLED EGGPLANT, TRI-COLOR PEPPERS, AND SUMMER SQUASH

GRILLED SAUSAGES AND TUSCAN BREAD

MARINATED GRILLED TUNA

GRILLED CHICKEN WITH ROASTED TOMATO SAUCE

SUMMER TOMATO SALAD

TUSCAN BREAD AND TOMATO SALAD

PEACHES IN CHIANTI

Grigliata di melanzane, peperoni tre colori, e zucchini

GRILLED EGGPLANT, TRI-COLOR PEPPERS, AND SUMMER SQUASH

**For the most visually appealing presentation, select the freshest-hued vegetables.
To make a more substantial antipasto, serve with smoked mozzarella.**

2 MEDIUM EGGPLANTS, PEELED AND CUT IN ¼-INCH SLICES

2 MEDIUM SUMMER SQUASH, CUT DIAGONALLY IN ½-INCH SLICES

2 RED BELL PEPPERS, CUT IN WEDGES

1 GREEN BELL PEPPER, CUT IN WEDGES

1 YELLOW BELL PEPPER, CUT IN WEDGES

½ CUP GARLIC-FLAVORED OLIVE OIL

¼ CUP CHOPPED FRESH BASIL

Preheat grill to medium.

Sprinkle eggplant slices with salt; place in a colander in the sink and allow to drain for 30 minutes. Rinse well, drain and pat dry.

Brush vegetables on all sides with olive oil. Grill eggplant 6-7 minutes per side, peppers about 7 minutes per side, and squash about 4 minutes per side. When vegetables are browned, transfer to serving platter. Sprinkle with basil just before serving. Serves 8-10.

Salsiccie alla griglia con pane toscano

GRILLED SAUSAGES AND TUSCAN BREAD

**This humble selection is nothing short of fabulous. Lightly brushing the sausage
with olive oil before grilling ensures that it won't stick to the grill.**

2 POUNDS SWEET OR HOT ITALIAN SAUSAGES

1 LARGE LOAF TUSCAN PEASANT BREAD, CUT INTO
1-INCH CUBES

¼ CUP EXTRA-VIRGIN OLIVE OIL

SALT AND FRESHLY GROUND BLACK PEPPER TO TASTE

1 TABLESPOON MINCED FRESH FLAT-LEAF ITALIAN PARSLEY

ROSEMARY SPRIGS FOR GARNISH

Preheat grill to medium.

Pierce sausages with a fork; place in boiling water and cook
for 10 minutes. Remove sausages and cut into 2-inch pieces.
Thread sausage and bread alternately onto skewers. In a small
bowl, combine olive oil, parsley, salt, and pepper. Brush skewered sausage and bread with olive oil mixture. Grill until
sausages and bread are medium browned. Remove from skewers and transfer to serving platter. Sprinkle with parsley just
before serving. Garnish with rosemary sprigs. Serves 8-10.

Tonno marinato alla griglia

MARINATED GRILLED TUNA

**This pesto marinade manages to improve on the already perfect taste of tender tuna
steaks. To ensure not overpowering the fish, marinate for less than an hour.**

1 CUP PREPARED PESTO SAUCE

½ CUP RED WINE VINEGAR

SALT AND FRESHLY GROUND BLACK PEPPER TO TASTE

2½ POUNDS TUNA STEAKS, CUT AT LEAST 1-INCH THICK

Pesto Sauce

⅓ CUP EXTRA-VIRGIN OLIVE OIL

2 CUPS FRESH BASIL LEAVES

4 CLOVES GARLIC

2 OUNCES PINE NUTS

3 TABLESPOONS GRATED PARMESAN

To prepare pesto sauce, put olive oil, basil, pine nuts, garlic,
and Parmesan in blender or food processor and blend
thoroughly.

In a medium bowl, combine pesto sauce, vinegar, salt, and
pepper; stir to mix thoroughly. Cut tuna steaks into 10 por-
tions (about 4 ounces each). Add tuna, cover, and marinate in
the refrigerator no more than 1 hour.

Preheat grill to medium.

Remove tuna from marinade. Grill about 4-5 minutes per
side or to desired degree of doneness. Serves 10.

Pollo alla griglia con salsa di pomodori arrosto

GRILLED CHICKEN WITH ROASTED TOMATO SAUCE

Charred tomatoes add a sweet-smoky flavor to the sauce—a hearty-tasting
accompaniment to the herb-marinated chicken.

6 BONELESS CHICKEN BREASTS (ABOUT 1½ POUNDS)

½ CUP LEMON JUICE

5 CLOVES GARLIC, SLICED

1 TABLESPOON RED WINE VINEGAR

2 TABLESPOONS CHOPPED FRESH ROSEMARY

½ CUP OLIVE OIL, DIVIDED

SALT AND FRESHLY GROUND BLACK PEPPER TO TASTE

4 MEDIUM TOMATOES, CUT IN HALF AND SEEDED

1 CUP OVEN-ROASTED GARLIC AND ONION SAUCE
(SEE RECIPE, P. 136)

¼ CUP CHOPPED FRESH BASIL

2 TABLESPOONS CHOPPED FRESH FLAT-LEAF ITALIAN PARSLEY

2 LARGE CLOVES GARLIC, CHOPPED

2 TEASPOONS GRATED LEMON ZEST

Place chicken in a bowl with lemon juice, garlic, vinegar, rosemary, 5 tablespoons olive oil, salt, and pepper. Marinate in the refrigerator several hours or overnight.

Preheat oven to 450° F.

Place tomatoes, cut side down, on a lightly greased baking sheet. Bake 20-25 minutes or until tomatoes char and soften. Place in a food processor bowl along with sauce, basil, parsley, garlic, 3 tablespoons olive oil, lemon zest, salt, and pepper. Pulse until smooth. Set aside. (Do not refrigerate.)

Preheat grill to medium.

Cut breasts in half and grill about 3-5 minutes per side or until thoroughly cooked. Serve with roasted tomato sauce. Serves 6-10.

Insalata estiva di pomodori

SUMMER TOMATO SALAD

**For the season's tomato aficionados, this simple salad is a little slice of heaven.
Select only sun-ripened tomatoes that are bright red and firm.**

8 FRESH RIPE TOMATOES, CORED

3 TABLESPOONS EXTRA-VIRGIN OLIVE OIL

¼ CUP MINCED FRESH FLAT-LEAF ITALIAN PARSLEY

¼ CUP MINCED FRESH BASIL

1 TABLESPOON FRESHLY GROUND BLACK PEPPER

SALT TO TASTE

Slice tomatoes into ½-inch slices. Arrange in a circular pattern on a serving platter. Drizzle with olive oil; sprinkle with herbs and pepper. Allow to marinate at room temperature at least 30 minutes. Season with salt and serve. Serves 10.

Panzanella

TUSCAN BREAD AND TOMATO SALAD

A delicious display of the reward of rejuvenating old and stale bread. Absorbing the vinegar's sharpness, the bread contrasts nicely with the vegetables' fresh flavors.

1½ POUNDS STALE PEASANT BREAD (PREFERABLY WHOLE WHEAT)

4 TABLESPOONS RED WINE VINEGAR

4 FRESH RIPE TOMATOES, COARSELY CHOPPED

2 SMALL RED ONIONS, QUARTERED AND THINLY SLICED

2 TABLESPOONS CHOPPED FRESH FLAT-LEAF ITALIAN PARSLEY

2 TABLESPOONS CHOPPED FRESH BASIL

⅓ CUP EXTRA-VIRGIN OLIVE OIL

SALT AND FRESHLY GROUND BLACK PEPPER TO TASTE

ROMAINE LETTUCE LEAVES

Slice bread and cut into 1-inch cubes; place in a large bowl and sprinkle with just enough water to moisten without making soggy. Sprinkle with vinegar; toss lightly to coat. Add tomatoes, onion, parsley, and basil. In a small bowl, combine olive oil, salt, and pepper; whisk until well blended. Pour over bread salad; toss to coat well. Adjust seasonings; add more vinegar, if needed. Refrigerate, covered, at least 30 minutes. To serve, line individual salad plates with lettuce leaves and top with salad. Serves 8-10.

Pesche al Chianti

PEACHES IN CHIANTI

**A beloved classic in Tuscany, probably because Chianti is the region's most renowned
wine. For best results, use dark pink peaches and a lighter-bodied Chianti.**

10 RIPE JUICY PEACHES

1 CUP CHIANTI WINE

10 AMARETTI BISCOTTI

Blanch peaches in boiling water 10-15 seconds, plunge into cold water; then peel. Cut in half and remove pit. Slice and place in a shallow bowl; pour in wine. Cover and chill at least 2 hours. Serve in individual dessert bowls with amaretti biscotti. Serves 10.

Autunno
FALL

AFTER THE HEADY DAYS OF SUMMER, FALL ARRIVES AS SOMETHING OF A RELIEF. COOLER WEATHER WAFTS IN, AND LIFE RESUMES A MORE NORMAL PACE. FALL MAY BE NATURE'S SWAN SONG, BUT IT CERTAINLY PUTS ON A SHOW. FOR STARTERS, THERE ARE THE WILD MUSHROOMS, WHOSE ARRIVAL IN TUSCAN MARKETS IS HERALDED AS A MOMENTOUS EVENT. *PORCINI* ARE THE FIRST ON VIEW IN EARLY FALL, FOLLOWED BY *PORTOBELLO*, *TROMBE DI MORTE* (WHITE OR BLACK CHANTERELLES), AND LATER, THE RARE BLACK TRUFFLES, TO NAME BUT A FEW. *CREMINI*—A POOR COUSIN TO THE PORCINI—ARE AVAILABLE YEAR-ROUND, SATISFY-ING NATIVE ITALIANS' CRAVINGS WHEN THE ALL-TOO-BRIEF PORCINI SEA-SON IS ENDED. TUSCANS ARE SO TAKEN WITH THEIR MEATY PORCINI THAT THEY SERVE THEM GRILLED—A DELICACY, PURE AND SIMPLE. (REMOVE

STEMS AND WIPE CAPS WITH A DAMP CLOTH. LIGHTLY BRUSH CAPS WITH EXTRA-VIRGIN OLIVE OIL, AND GRILL FOR THREE MINUTES ON EACH SIDE. SERVE HOT, DRIZZLED WITH OLIVE OIL AND SEASONED WITH SALT AND PEPPER.)

PRODUCE STANDS ARE ALSO RIFE WITH END-OF-SUMMER SWISS CHARD AND RED BELL PEPPERS, JOINED LATER BY FENNEL, SQUASH, AND A VARIETY OF LUSCIOUS APPLES AND PEARS. THE GRAPE HARVEST IN ITALY RUNS BETWEEN MID-SEPTEMBER AND THE END OF OCTOBER. BUT NOWHERE IS IT CELEBRATED AS PASSIONATELY AS IN THE TOWN OF GREVE IN CHIANTI, WHERE PARADES, WINE TASTINGS, CONCERTS, AND DANCES FILL UP A FIVE-DAY FESTIVAL.

THEN COMES THE OLIVE HARVEST, YIELDING SOME OF THE MOST AROMATIC AND FLAVORFUL OLIVE OIL IN THE COUNTRY. THE ANNUAL FIRST PRESSING OF OLIVES, WHICH PRODUCES THE OLIVE OIL DESIGNATED EXTRA-VIRGIN, IS ALWAYS GREETED WITH GREAT ENTHUSIASM—PARTICULARLY IN LUCCA, A CITY FAMOUS FOR SUPPLYING THE FINEST OLIVE OIL. WITH AN INTENSE, FRUITY FLAVOR AND GREENISH-GOLDEN HUE, *OLIO EXTRAVERGINE D'OLIVA* IS SOMETHING NO TUSCAN COOK COULD LIVE WITHOUT. IN FACT, BUTTER IS VERY SELDOM USED IN TUSCAN DISHES.

AS THE WEATHER TURNS COOLER, MEALS IN TUSCANY TAKE ON MORE SUBSTANCE. MORE WARMED ANTIPASTI ARE IN ORDER, AND THERE'S A PRONOUNCED EMPHASIS ON ROASTED OR BAKED VEGETABLE SIDE DISHES. SUBSTANTIVE DINING, HOWEVER, DOESN'T PRECLUDE HAVING FUN WITH THE SEASON'S ENTERTAINING, WHICH IS WHY YOU'LL FIND A CREATIVE PARTY MENU FEATURING GOURMET PIZZAS—FOR THE GROWN-UP PALATE.

Pizza da gran sera

Sophisticated Pizza Party (Serves 8 to 10)

Who says kids have a lock on pizza parties? And never mind that pizza is not authentic Tuscan cuisine. These specialty pies will satisfy the most discerning palates (Tuscans' included). And making the crust from scratch is a must. Choose one pie or serve all three—either way, there's little chance you'll be looking at leftovers.

CLAM-STUFFED MUSHROOMS

SPINACH OLIVE PIZZA

WILD MUSHROOM PIZZA

CREAMY ROASTED RED PEPPER PIZZA WITH SHRIMP

PEAR AND FENNEL SALAD

ORANGES IN MARSALA GLAZE

Caponata al forno

CLAM-STUFFED MUSHROOMS

A savory antipasto anytime, this makes an especially ideal appetizer here.
While the pizzas are being prepared, your guests will be enjoyably occupied.

16-20 LARGE FRESH MUSHROOMS FOR STUFFING

3 CLOVES GARLIC, MINCED

¼ CUP OLIVE OIL

1 CAN (6½ OZ.) MINCED CLAMS, DRAINED

2 CUPS FRESH BREAD CRUMBS

2 TABLESPOONS GRATED PARMESAN CHEESE

2 TABLESPOONS MINCED FRESH FLAT-LEAF ITALIAN PARSLEY

½ TEASPOON OREGANO

½ TEASPOON SALT

¼ TEASPOON FRESHLY GROUND BLACK PEPPER

MINCED FRESH PARSLEY FOR GARNISH

Preheat oven to 450° F.

Wipe mushrooms with a cloth to remove any loose dirt. Remove stems and chop finely. In a large skillet, sauté garlic and chopped mushrooms stems in olive oil. Add clams, bread crumbs, Parmesan, parsley, oregano, salt, and pepper; mix thoroughly. Lightly grease a baking sheet with olive oil. Fill mushroom caps with stuffing, mounding slightly in center; arrange on baking sheet. Bake about 12-15 minutes or until golden. Arrange mushrooms on platter. Garnish with parsley. Serves 8-10.

Pizza agli spinaci e olive

SPINACH OLIVE PIZZA

**This nicely exotic-flavored pie is evocative of everything Mediterranean.
For olive lovers, double the amount of black olives.**

2 SMALL UNBAKED PIZZA CRUSTS (SEE RECIPE, P. 80)

1 CUP FRESH TOMATO BASIL SAUCE (SEE RECIPE, P. 136), DIVIDED

1 CUP COOKED SPINACH, DIVIDED

1 CUP SHREDDED MOZZARELLA CHEESE

½ CUP SLIVERED OIL-CURED BLACK OLIVES

Preheat oven to 475° F.

Prepare pizza dough as directed, shaping into two crusts. Top each crust with ½ cup sauce, ½ cup cooked spinach, ½ cup mozzarella, and ¼ cup slivered olives. Bake about 15 minutes or until crust is golden brown. Serves 4-8.

Crosta semplice per pizza

BASIC PIZZA CRUST

Sponge:

¼ CUP LUKEWARM WATER

1 PACKAGE ACTIVE DRY YEAST

¼ CUP BREAD FLOUR

Dough:

½ CUP LUKEWARM WATER

1 TABLESPOON MILK

2 TABLESPOONS OLIVE OIL

½ TEASPOON SALT

1¾ CUPS UNBLEACHED FLOUR

ADDITIONAL FLOUR FOR KNEADING

CORNMEAL (OPTIONAL)

In a small bowl, make the sponge by combining the first three ingredients. With a wooden spoon, stir to mix well; cover bowl with a towel and allow to sit 25 to 30 minutes. To this add ½ cup warm water, milk, olive oil, salt, and flour. Mix thoroughly until a ball of dough forms. On a floured surface, knead the dough 10 to 15 minutes, adding more flour as needed. Place dough in an oiled bowl. Cover and place bowl in a warm place. Let dough rise until double in size, about 2 hours. Punch dough down. Allow dough to rise again, about 45 minutes to 1 hour. Dough is now ready to shape, top, and bake. If desired, sprinkle cornmeal on baking pan before shaping pizza dough. Makes 1 large or 2 small pizza crusts.

Pizza ai funghi di bosco

WILD MUSHROOM PIZZA

For smokier flavor, select porcini and portobello mushrooms. For something more subtle, mix several wild and tame mushrooms, including cremini, chanterelles, and oyster mushrooms.

2 SMALL UNBAKED PIZZA CRUSTS (SEE RECIPE, P. 80)

8 OUNCES WILD MUSHROOMS, SLICED

1 TABLESPOON OLIVE OIL

1 CUP MARINARA SAUCE WITH BURGUNDY WINE (SEE RECIPE, P. 137), DIVIDED

1 CUP SHREDDED MOZZARELLA CHEESE, DIVIDED

Preheat oven to 475° F.

Prepare pizza dough as directed, shaping into two crusts.

In a large skillet, sauté mushrooms in olive oil until lightly browned. Top each crust with ½ cup sauce, half the sautéed mushrooms, and ½ cup mozzarella. Bake about 15 minutes or until crust is golden brown. Serves 4-8.

Pizza bianca ai peperoni arrosto con gamberi

CREAMY ROASTED RED PEPPER PIZZA WITH SHRIMP

Here's a rich pie sure to be a crowd-pleaser. And this delicious topping goes great over
***orzo* for a light pasta course.**

2 SMALL UNBAKED PIZZA CRUSTS (SEE RECIPE, P. 80)

1 CUP CREAMY ALFREDO SAUCE (SEE RECIPE, P. 138)

1 JAR (7 OZ.) ROASTED RED PEPPERS, DRAINED AND PUREED

1 CUP SHREDDED MOZZARELLA CHEESE, DIVIDED

8 OUNCES COOKED SHRIMP

2 TABLESPOONS FRESH BASIL, THINLY SLICED

Preheat oven to 475° F.

Prepare pizza dough as directed, shaping into two crusts.

In a bowl, combine Alfredo sauce with roasted pepper puree. Top each crust with ½ cup sauce mixture and ½ cup mozarella; sprinkle each with basil. Bake about 10 minutes or until crust is lightly golden; top with shrimp and bake another 5-6 minutes. Serves 4-8.

Insalata di pere e finocchio
PEAR AND FENNEL SALAD

Fennel lends a delicate anise flavor to this mixed-greens salad.
Topping it with pear slices adds a sweet, and pretty, touch.

3 MEDIUM FENNEL BULBS, CORED AND CUT INTO THIN SLICES

8 CUPS MIXED SALAD GREENS (RED LEAF LETTUCE, BIBB, BOSTON, RADICCHIO)

SALT AND FRESHLY GROUND BLACK PEPPER TO TASTE

⅓ CUP EXTRA-VIRGIN OLIVE OIL

JUICE OF 1 LEMON

3 OR 4 RED BARTLETT OR BOSC PEARS, CORED AND THINLY SLICED

In a large bowl, combine fennel slices with salad greens; chill. Combine salt, pepper, olive oil, and lemon juice. When ready to serve, toss chilled greens with dressing. Serve on individual salad plates. Top with pear slices. Serves 8-10.

ORANGES IN MARSALA GLAZE

An especially easy, even elegant, dessert. Use a sweet Superiore Marsala for
the most luscious results.

PEEL OF 1 ORANGE, CUT INTO VERY THIN STRIPS

10 LARGE ORANGES

½ CUP SUGAR

1½ CUPS MARSALA WINE

½ CUP COINTREAU

In a small saucepan with boiling water, simmer orange-peel
strips over medium heat 5 minutes; drain and set aside.

Slice ends from oranges; remove peel and all white pith.
Separate each orange into sections, removing all membrane
between sections. Place sectioned oranges in a large bowl;
cover and chill.

In a medium saucepan, combine sugar, wine, and liqueur.
Bring to a boil; cover and cook over medium heat until mixture is reduced by half and becomes syrupy. Add orange-peel
strips and chill for at least 2 hours. To serve, spoon orange sections into individual dessert dishes. Top with marsala glaze.
Serves 10.

Cena simpatica

Simpatica Supper (Serves 4)

This selection turns ordinary dinnertime into a memorable meal. The best part: it's as easy to create as it is enjoyable. For hearty appetites, go with the veal stew. But if the family's demanding pasta, they'll relish the fettucine entree. The salad is a celebration of flavorful greens. And the very special dessert is a seasonal classic.

PORCINI BRUSCHETTA

SAVORY VEAL STEW WITH COUSCOUS

OR

FETTUCCINE WITH VEAL AND SPINACH

ESCAROLE AND CHICORY SALAD WITH SHAVED PARMESAN

CRANBERRY WALNUT TART

Bruschetta ai funghi porcini

PORCINI BRUSCHETTA

The savory mushroom topping makes this antipasto practically a meal in itself.

8 OUNCES PORCINI OR CREMINI MUSHROOMS, THINLY SLICED

1 TABLESPOON PORCINI-INFUSED OIL

½ LOAF CRUSTY TUSCAN BREAD, CUT INTO 8-12 SLICES (ABOUT ¾-INCH THICK)

3 CLOVES GARLIC, CRUSHED

EXTRA-VIRGIN OLIVE OIL

FRESH BASIL, THINLY SLICED FOR GARNISH (OPTIONAL)

Preheat broiler.

In a large skillet, sauté mushrooms in porcini oil just until they begin to release their juices. Remove from heat; cover to keep warm. Toast or broil bread slices on both sides until lightly browned. While still warm, rub one side with crushed garlic and drizzle liberally with olive oil. Top with sautéed mushrooms. Serve immediately. Garnish with fresh basil, if desired. Makes 8-12 pieces.

Spezzatino di vitello con cuscus

SAVORY VEAL STEW WITH COUSCOUS

One of Tuscan cuisine's most popular meats, veal is deliciously showcased in
this satisfying stew. Serving over couscous (or orzo) nicely lightens this dish.

2 TABLESPOONS OLIVE OIL

1½ POUNDS VEAL STEW MEAT, CUT INTO BITE-SIZE PIECES

SALT AND FRESHLY GROUND BLACK PEPPER TO TASTE

1 CUP CHOPPED ONIONS

2 CARROTS, CUT IN HALF LENGTHWISE AND SLICED

2 CLOVES GARLIC, MINCED

1 SMALL GREEN BELL PEPPER, DICED

1 MEDIUM ZUCCHINI, QUARTERED AND SLICED

1 LARGE BAKING POTATO, PEELED AND DICED

1 CUP CANNED GARBANZO BEANS, DRAINED AND RINSED

3 CUPS MARINARA SAUCE WITH BURGUNDY WINE
(SEE RECIPE, P. 137)

½ CUP BEEF BROTH

1 TEASPOON DRIED BASIL

4 CUPS STEAMED COUSCOUS

In a large saucepan or Dutch oven, heat olive oil. Add stew
meat and brown well over high heat. Season with salt and pepper. With a slotted spoon, remove meat and set aside. In the
same pan, lightly sauté onions, carrots, garlic, pepper, and zucchini. Add potato, garbanzo beans, marinara sauce, broth, and
basil. Return meat to saucepan. Bring to a boil; reduce heat
and simmer, covered 1 hour or until meat is very tender. Stir
occasionally. Serve in deep bowls over steamed couscous.
Serves 4-6.

Fettuccine con fettine di vitello e spinaci

FETTUCCINE WITH VEAL AND SPINACH

**A luscious harmony of mellow flavors, this dish manages to be rich without
being particularly heavy—making it ideal for informal dining.**

1 POUND VEAL CUTLETS, POUNDED THIN (ABOUT 12 PIECES)

1 TABLESPOON LEMON JUICE

¼ CUP MINCED FRESH FLAT-LEAF ITALIAN PARSLEY

2 TABLESPOONS GRATED PARMESAN CHEESE

2 TABLESPOONS OLIVE OIL

6 OUNCES SLICED ASSORTED MUSHROOMS (SUCH AS SHIITAKE,
CREMINI, OR OYSTER)

2 CUPS CREAMY ALFREDO SAUCE (SEE RECIPE, P. 138)

1 PACKAGE (9 OZ.) FRESH FETTUCCINE

2 CUPS FRESH SPINACH, TRIMMED AND COARSELY CHOPPED

Sprinkle veal pieces with lemon juice, parsley, and cheese. Roll
jelly-roll style into small rolls. Secure with toothpicks or
string. In a large skillet, brown veal rolls in olive oil on all
sides. Remove and set aside.

In the same skillet, sauté mushrooms until lightly browned.
Return veal rolls to skillet. Add Alfredo sauce. Cover and sim-
mer over low heat 10 minutes, stirring occasionally.
Meanwhile, cook fettuccine according to package directions.

Drain pasta; immediately toss hot pasta with spinach
leaves. Spoon sauce over pasta; toss to coat well. Serve veal
rolls over pasta. Serves 4.

Insalata di scarola e cicoria con scaglie di Parmigiano

ESCAROLE AND CHICORY SALAD WITH SHAVED PARMESAN

**This salad of assertive greens pairs well with subtly flavored main courses.
Don't scrimp on the Parmesan—the shavings practically melt in your mouth.**

1 SMALL HEAD CHICORY, TRIMMED AND TORN INTO BITE-SIZE PIECES (ABOUT 4 CUPS)

1 SMALL HEAD ESCAROLE, TRIMMED AND CUT INTO BITE-SIZE PIECES (ABOUT 4 CUPS)

3 TABLESPOONS EXTRA-VIRGIN OLIVE OIL

1 TABLESPOON BALSAMIC VINEGAR

1 TEASPOON DIJON MUSTARD

SALT AND PEPPER TO TASTE

8 OUNCES RED OR YELLOW CHERRY TOMATOES FOR GARNISH

SHAVED PARMESAN CHEESE FOR GARNISH

Place greens in a large bowl. In a small jar with tight-fitting lid, combine olive oil, balsamic vinegar, mustard, salt, and pepper; shake until well blended. Spoon dressing over salad; toss to coat well. Serve salad on individual salad plates. Garnish with cherry tomatoes and shaved Parmesan cheese. Serves 4.

Crostata di noci e mirtilli rossi

CRANBERRY WALNUT TART

**Sweet-tart cranberries give this seasonal confection sophisticated appeal.
If fresh berries aren't available, frozen will work just as beautifully.**

Dough

1 CUP FLOUR

2 TABLESPOONS SUGAR

¼ TEASPOON SALT

4 TABLESPOONS COLD UNSALTED BUTTER, CUT IN CUBES

½ TEASPOON FINELY GRATED LEMON RIND

2½ TABLESPOONS ICE WATER

In a food processor, combine flour, sugar, and salt. Pulse briefly to combine. Add chilled butter and lemon rind, pulse 10 to 12 times or until butter mixture resembles coarse oatmeal. With food processor running, add ice water all at once. Process for about 10 seconds until a ball of dough forms. Turn dough onto a sheet of plastic wrap. Flatten to form a 7-inch circle. Wrap dough tightly and refrigerate at least 1 hour.

Filling:

2 CUPS CRANBERRIES

½ CUP CHOPPED WALNUTS

3 TABLESPOONS SUGAR

2 TABLESPOONS BROWN SUGAR

CONFECTIONERS' SUGAR

Preheat oven to 450° F.

Roll dough into an 11-inch circle on a lightly floured surface. Place dough on a baking sheet. In a large bowl, thoroughly combine cranberries, walnuts, sugar, and brown sugar.

Spoon cranberry mixture over crust, leaving about a 1½-inch border around the outside edge. Fold dough over cranberries, pinching as necessary to keep it in place. Bake 15-18 minutes, or until crust is golden and berries are juicy. Cool on a rack about 10 minutes. Dust with sifted confectioners' sugar. Serve warm. Serves 6-8.

Tavolata per la festa della vendemmia

Grape Harvest Festival Meal (Serves 6 to 8)

Start a new tradition of celebrating this native Italian *festa*. Or simply employ this menu of specialty fare whenever you're in the mood for some serious entertaining. The eye-catching antipasto is an inspired take on crostini. For the first course, there are two lovely and aromatic choices. The beef tenderloin makes an impressive secondo. And topping it all off, an all-time classic that is nothing short of sublime.

POLENTA CROSTINI WITH HERBED GOAT CHEESE

GRANDMOTHER'S KERCHIEFS

OR

ORZO WITH BUTTERNUT SQUASH AND CIPOLLINE

HERB-ROASTED BEEF TENDERLOIN

BAKED FENNEL WITH PARMIGIANO-REGGIANO

TUSCAN ZABAGLIONE WITH GRAPES

Crostini di polenta con formaggio di capra

POLENTA CROSTINI WITH HERBED GOAT CHEESE

These golden toasts topped with the most delightfully tart cheese elevate antipasto to an art form. Wait till guests arrive to broil a second time; these are best served warm.

1 CUP POLENTA OR COARSE CORNMEAL

4 CUPS BOILING WATER

2 TABLESPOONS GRATED PARMESAN CHEESE

2 TABLESPOONS MINCED FRESH FLAT-LEAF ITALIAN PARSLEY

2 TABLESPOONS MINCED FRESH BASIL

EXTRA-VIRGIN OLIVE OIL

6 OUNCES HERBED GOAT CHEESE, CRUMBLED

Slowly pour polenta into boiling water, stirring to keep smooth. Cook over low heat, stirring constantly, 3-5 minutes or until polenta thickens. Remove from heat and stir in Parmesan, parsley and basil. Spoon mixture evenly into a lightly oiled, shallow baking pan; allow to cool. When thoroughly cooled, cut into squares, then slice each diagonally into two triangles. Lightly brush both sides with olive oil. Arrange on a broiler pan. Place under broiler and cook until crisp, about 4 minutes per side. Evenly top each with crumbled goat cheese and return to broiler for 1 minute. Serve immediately. Makes 36 crostini.

Four Secrets to Perfect Polenta

Secret #1: The cornmeal doesn't have to be added to boiling water. Prevent a scalding episode by adding the meal to a pot of cool water, a handful at a time, and stir vigorously with a wire whisk. Then set the pot over medium heat, and continue stirring.

Secret #2: Once the cornmeal starts to thicken, turn heat to low and switch from the whisk to a wooden spoon for stirring.

Secret #3: A recipe's timing is one thing, but you'll know the polenta is definitely done once the meal pulls entirely away from the sides of the pot.

Secret #4: The finer the meal, the quicker it will cook. Coarse-ground cornmeal can take up to an hour; finely ground, as little as 20 minutes.

GRANDMOTHER'S KERCHIEFS

These charmingly named stuffed-pasta squares make a rich, delicious, and rather
elaborate selection. For an appreciative audience, they're worth the effort.

Filling:

2½ POUNDS FRESH SPINACH, THOROUGHLY RINSED WITH STEMS
REMOVED (OR 2 PACKAGES [10 OZ. EACH] FROZEN CHOPPED
SPINACH)

1 POUND RICOTTA CHEESE

2 EXTRA-LARGE EGGS

1 CUP GRATED PARMESAN CHEESE

SALT AND PEPPER TO TASTE

FRESHLY GROUND NUTMEG TO TASTE

Balsamella:

4 OUNCES SWEET BUTTER

¼ CUP UNBLEACHED FLOUR

3½ CUPS MILK, HEATED

PINCH OF SALT

16 SQUARES (6" × 6") FRESH PASTA SHEETS

3 CUPS OVEN-ROASTED GARLIC AND ONION SAUCE
(SEE RECIPE, P. 136)

FRESH BASIL LEAVES FOR GARNISH

Cook spinach briefly in a small amount of water until spinach wilts. Place in a strainer; squeeze out excess water. Chop spinach and place in a large bowl. Add ricotta cheese, eggs, Parmesan cheese, salt, pepper, and nutmeg. Mix thoroughly and set aside. To prepare the balsamella, melt butter over low heat in a saucepan. Whisk in flour until smooth. Cook about 2 minutes over low heat. Add heated milk and salt to flour mixture. Continue to cook until sauce thickens, stirring frequently. Remove from heat.

Bring a large saucepan with salted water to a rapid boil. Drop pasta sheets in boiling water, one at a time. Cook each 10 to 15 seconds (pasta will just float to the top of the water). Removed cooked pasta and place immediately in a large bowl of cold water to which 2 tablespoons olive oil have been added. Continue until all pasta is cooked and cooled.

Preheat oven to 375° F.

Place pasta sheets on clean kitchen towels; blot to drain well. Spoon 2 heaping tablespoons spinach filling onto the center of the pasta square. Fold to make a triangle. Fold outer points in to meet in center. Place "kerchiefs" in a buttered baking dish in a single layer with points facing the center. Spoon balsamella sauce over pasta. Bake 20 minutes or until bubbly. While pasta is baking, heat Oven-Roasted Garlic Sauce in a saucepan. Serve 2 filled pasta kerchiefs on each plate. Top with heated sauce. Garnish with a fresh basil leaf. Serves 8.

Orzo alla zucca e cipolline

ORZO WITH BUTTERNUT SQUASH AND CIPOLLINE

Orzo, a mini pasta (and a step up from rice), is the perfect backdrop for this
complementary blend of sweet squash and bittersweet Italian onions.

2 TABLESPOONS BUTTER

2 TABLESPOONS OLIVE OIL

2 CUPS THINLY SLICED CIPOLLINE (OR 2 LARGE ONIONS)

4 TO 4½ CUPS DICED, PEELED BUTTERNUT SQUASH
(ABOUT 1½ POUNDS)

1 TABLESPOON CHOPPED FRESH SAGE

SALT AND FRESHLY GROUND BLACK PEPPER TO TASTE

ABOUT 5½ CUPS CHICKEN BROTH
(HOMEMADE OR CANNED), HEATED

1 POUND ORZO

3 TABLESPOONS MINCED FRESH FLAT-LEAF ITALIAN PARSLEY

1 CUP GRATED PARMESAN CHEESE

In a large saucepan, melt butter with olive oil over low heat.
Add cipollini and sauté about 5 minutes, until translucent.
Add squash, sage, salt, and pepper. Add about 1 cup hot broth
and simmer, covered, about 10 to 15 minutes or until squash is
tender.

Stir in orzo and 4 cups hot broth. Simmer and cook, uncovered, stirring frequently to prevent sticking until pasta is
al dente and liquid is absorbed (about 10 minutes). Add additional ½ cup broth, if necessary. Mixture should have a creamy
consistency. Cover, remove from heat, and let stand 5 minutes.
Stir in parsley and cheese. Serve immediately. Serves 6-8.

Filetto di manzo arrosto alle erbe
HERB-ROASTED BEEF TENDERLOIN

An aromatic marinade enhances the velvetiness of this quick-roasting cut of meat, while a savory woodsy-flavored sauce ensures its moistness.

1 WHOLE BEEF TENDERLOIN (ABOUT 5 POUNDS, TRIMMED)

2 TABLESPOONS ROSEMARY-FLAVORED OLIVE OIL

1 TEASPOON SALT

1 TEASPOON FRESHLY GROUND BLACK PEPPER

3 CLOVES GARLIC, MINCED

2 TABLESPOONS MINCED FRESH FLAT-LEAF ITALIAN PARSLEY

PORCINI MUSHROOM SAUCE

Evenly rub beef tenderloin with olive oil. Season all surfaces of meat with salt, pepper, garlic and parsley. Wrap roast with plastic wrap and marinate at least 4 hours or overnight.

Preheat oven to 425° F.

Place meat in a shallow baking pan. Roast 45-55 minutes or until internal temperature of meat reaches 130° F for rare. Meanwhile, prepare Porcini Mushroom Sauce. Let roast stand about 5 minutes before carving. Serve with Porcini Mushroom Sauce. Serves 8.

Porcini Mushroom Sauce

1 PACKAGE (25 GRAMS) DRIED PORCINI MUSHROOMS

2 CUPS WATER

3 TABLESPOONS UNSALTED BUTTER

¼ CUP BURGUNDY WINE

½ CUP OVEN-ROASTED GARLIC AND ONION SAUCE (SEE RECIPE, P. 136)

3 TABLESPOONS LIGHT CREAM

½ TEASPOON SALT

FRESHLY GROUND BLACK PEPPER TO TASTE

In a small saucepan, combine porcini with water; simmer 20 minutes over low heat. Drain mushrooms and reserve liquid. In a skillet, sauté mushrooms in butter; set aside. Simmer mushroom liquid and wine 15 minutes or until reduced to 1 cup. Add sautéed mushrooms and sauce; heat gently. Remove from heat and add cream, salt, and pepper; stir thoroughly.

Finocchio al forno con Parmigiano-Reggiano
BAKED FENNEL WITH PARMIGIANO-REGGIANO

The fennel's delicate anise flavor actually sweetens when cooked. Topping with this extraordinary variety of sharp Parmesan makes for an exquisite taste sensation.

4-6 FENNEL BULBS, QUARTERED

2 TABLESPOONS BUTTER, CUT IN PIECES

1 TABLESPOON MINCED FRESH FLAT-LEAF ITALIAN PARSLEY, DIVIDED

1 TABLESPOON MINCED FRESH SAGE, DIVIDED

SALT AND FRESHLY GROUND BLACK PEPPER TO TASTE

¼ CUP CHICKEN BROTH, HOMEMADE OR CANNED

½ CUP GRATED PARMIGIANO-REGGIANO CHEESE

Preheat oven to 350° F.

In a large saucepan, cook fennel in boiling salted water 5 minutes; drain and pat dry. Lightly oil a baking dish; layer with half of the fennel. Dot with butter. Season fennel with half of the parsley, sage, salt, and pepper. Top with remaining fennel and seasonings. Pour broth over fennel and sprinkle with cheese. Cover and bake 45 minutes. Increase oven temperature to 400° F. Uncover and bake 10 minutes longer or until golden brown. Serves 6-8.

Tips for Selecting Fennel

A staple in Tuscany that's attracting a following here, fennel, or *finocchio*, is an aromatic plant with a broad, bulbous base. Its seeds are used as a spice, and its feathery leaves as an herb. The bulb possesses a sweet, delicate flavor reminiscent of anise.

• Choose crisp pale-green bulbs that feel heavy and are free of any brown shading. The feathery foliage should be bright green.

• Fennel can be kept fresh for up to five days.

• For maximum shelf life, store tightly wrapped in a plastic bag, and refrigerate.

Zabaglione alla toscana con uva

TUSCAN ZABAGLIONE WITH GRAPES

**Such simple indulgence! Here, the Tuscan take on this Italian favorite—made with Vin Santo,
Tuscany's trademark dessert wine. For sheer perfection, use a medium-sweet Vin Santo.**

6 LARGE EGG YOLKS

6 TABLESPOONS SUGAR

½ CUP VIN SANTO

CHAMPAGNE GRAPES FOR GARNISH

In the top of a double boiler, place egg yolks and sugar; beat until pale yellow, thick, and creamy using a portable mixer or wire whisk. Place pan over several inches of boiling water. Add wine; beat about 4-5 minutes or until mixture forms a smooth custard. Spoon zabaglione into stemmed dessert dishes; garnish with grapes. Serve while still warm. Serves 4-6.

Inverno
WINTER

It has to be Mother Nature's cruelest joke: winter, which

offers the fewest raw materials of any season for making

effortless meals, happens to be the one most closely linked to

hearty eating. This is the time of year when Tuscans desire

warming, soothing, rib-sticking fare—not unlike those of us

here who know the true meaning of wind-chill factor. That

explains why stews, roasts, piping-hot pasta dishes, and soups you

can practically eat with a fork are mainstays of the cold-

weather kitchen. And while nature's bounty may be slim(mer)

pickings, the brilliance of *cucina toscana* is making the most of

what produce does crop up. Cabbage, potatoes, carrots, and

cauliflower appear regularly in winter dishes—and always in

SAVORY FASHION. REPRESENTING SALAD GREENS, RADICCHIO IS AT ITS PEAK BEGINNING MID-SEASON. FALL'S APPLES AND PEARS ARE THE BASIS FOR WINTER DESSERTS, WHICH TUSCAN COOKS CREATIVELY AUGMENT WITH NUTS AND SPICES FOR DELECTABLE CONFECTIONS THAT DON'T DISAPPOINT. AND FILLING IN THE CULINARY GAPS ARE BEANS AND LENTILS—YEAR-ROUND STAPLES OF TUSCAN CUISINE—WHICH DEMONSTRATE THEIR REMARKABLE VERSATILITY THIS SEASON IN SOUPS, SALADS, ANTIPASTI, AND MAIN COURSES ALIKE.

THE BEAUTY OF SERVING MORE ROBUST FARE IS THAT APPETITES ARE SATED WITH FEWER COURSES. IN FACT, SOME MEALS SUFFICE QUITE SATISFYINGLY WITH JUST ONE DISH—AS YOU'LL DISCOVER WITH MANY OF THE RECIPES IN THE FOLLOWING MENUS. OF COURSE, HOLIDAY DINING IS IN A CATEGORY UNTO ITSELF, AND THE CELEBRATORY BRUNCH MENU THAT ENDS THIS CHAPTER IS TO BE SAVORED FROM SOUP TO NUTS (OR IN THIS CASE, FROM CROSTINI TO BISCOTTI).

THE HOLIDAYS IN TUSCANY ARE OBSERVED WITH CENTURIES-OLD RITUALS. BUT THERE, AS HERE, THE REJOICING IS SHARED WITH LARGE GATHERINGS OF LOVED ONES—RELATED AND OTHERWISE. SO AS NATURE SETTLES IN FOR ITS LONG WINTER'S NAP, INDULGE IN THE WARMTH OF FAMILY AND FRIENDS, RELISH THE SEASON'S OFFERINGS, AND TAKE COMFORT IN THE KNOWLEDGE THAT, SPRING WILL ARRIVE ON CUE, AS ALWAYS, TO USHER IN THE NATURAL CYCLE OF LIFE ALL OVER AGAIN.

Cena alla buona in cucina

Cozy Kitchen Supper (Serves 6)

This selection works equally well as a restorative cold-weather supper for the family or as a casual Saturday night dinner for close friends. The sumptuous ribollita, Tuscany's famous bread soup, is practically a meal in itself. For the second course, opt for the orecchiette when catering to lighter appetites. However, when the crowd calls for extra-comforting fare, this special spinach lasagna will be most appreciated. And for a sweet and light finale, try this (nearly) effortless dessert.

TUSCAN BREAD SOUP

ORECCHIETTE WITH GREENS AND BEANS

OR

SPINACH ALFREDO LASAGNA

WILTED ESCAROLE WITH RAISINS AND PINE NUTS

POACHED PEARS

Ribollita

TUSCAN BREAD SOUP

The secret to this hearty and incredibly satisfying soup: allow mixture to cool and thicken long enough that it begs to be eaten with a fork.

⅔ CUP OLIVE OIL

1 LARGE ONION, CHOPPED

½ CUP CHOPPED CELERY

2 TABLESPOONS CHOPPED FRESH SAGE

2 CUPS OVEN-ROASTED GARLIC AND ONION SAUCE (SEE RECIPE, P. 136)

5 CUPS LOWER-SALT CHICKEN OR BEEF BROTH, HEATED (AS NEEDED)

SALT AND FRESHLY GROUND BLACK PEPPER TO TASTE

1 POUND SAVOY CABBAGE, CUT INTO ½-INCH STRIPS

2 ALL-PURPOSE POTATOES, PEELED AND CUBED

1 CUP COOKED (OR CANNED) CANNELLINI BEANS, DRAINED

6 THICK SLICES CRUSTY TUSCAN BREAD, PREFERABLY STALE

In a large stock pot, heat olive oil; add onion, celery, and sage and sauté lightly about 5 minutes. Stir in sauce and 4 cups hot broth, and season with salt and pepper. Add cabbage and potatoes; bring to a boil. Reduce heat to low and cook about 40 minutes, adding broth as needed. Soup should be rather thick. Add beans; simmer 5 minutes longer. Meanwhile, toast bread slices; cut into chunks.

Remove soup from heat; add bread chunks and stir to mix well. Let soup stand for 30 minutes, then refrigerate until cool (or overnight). To serve, reheat and simmer for 30 minutes. Serve in individual rimmed bowls; drizzle with olive oil before serving. Serves 6.

Orecchiette con spinaci e fagioli cannellini
ORECCHIETTE WITH GREENS AND BEANS

These pasta shapes are the perfect receptacles for this dish's riches. Bacon
provides a delicately smoky essence; spinach mellows when cooked.

1½ CUPS FRESH TOMATO BASIL SAUCE (SEE RECIPE, P. 136)

1 PACKAGE (10 OZ.) FRESH SPINACH

4 SLICES BACON, CHOPPED

3 CLOVES GARLIC, MINCED

1 SMALL ONION, CHOPPED

1 CAN (16 OZ.) WHITE BEANS, DRAINED AND RINSED

1 POUND ORECCHIETTE OR SHELL PASTA, COOKED AND
DRAINED

In a medium saucepan, heat sauce thoroughly; set aside.
Thoroughly wash spinach in cold water; remove and discard
stems. Tear spinach leaves coarsely; set aside. In a large skillet,
cook bacon until crisp; drain fat. In the same skillet; sauté garlic and onion until tender. Add beans; cook over low heat until
heated through, stirring occasionally.

Add spinach to skillet; cover and cook just until spinach is
wilted. Toss cooked pasta with heated sauce. Top with spinach
and bean mixture; lightly toss to coat. Serves 6.

Lasagne alla fiorentina
SPINACH ALFREDO LASAGNA

**Spinach elevates this crowd-pleasing standard to superior status. The addition of creamy
Alfredo sauce gives it a rich, new twist.**

1¼ POUNDS FRESH SPINACH, THOROUGHLY RINSED WITH STEMS
REMOVED (OR 1 PACKAGE [10 OZ.] FROZEN CHOPPED SPINACH,
THAWED AND SQUEEZED DRY

2 POUNDS PART-SKIM RICOTTA CHEESE

8 OUNCES SHREDDED PART-SKIM MOZZARELLA CHEESE

½ CUP GRATED PARMESAN CHEESE, DIVIDED

2 EGGS

SALT AND FRESHLY GROUND BLACK PEPPER TO TASTE

2¾ CUPS FRESH TOMATO BASIL SAUCE (SEE RECIPE, P. 136)

1 POUND LASAGNA NOODLES, COOKED AND DRAINED

1 CUP CREAMY ALFREDO SAUCE (SEE RECIPE, P. 138)

Preheat oven to 375° F.

In a large bowl, thoroughly combine spinach, ricotta, mozzarella, ¼ cup Parmesan, eggs, salt, and pepper. Pour ¾ cup tomato basil sauce evenly in a 13 × 9-inch baking dish. Layer four lasagna noodles over sauce. Spread half the spinach-cheese mixture over noodles. Top with 1 cup tomato sauce. Repeat layers, ending with lasagna noodles. Evenly spread Alfredo sauce over the top; sprinkle with remaining Parmesan. Cover and bake 1 hour. Uncover, bake another 10 minutes or until bubbly. Allow lasagna to sit 10 minutes before serving. Serves 6-8.

Scarola tiepida con uvetta e pinoli
WILTED ESCAROLE WITH RAISINS AND PINE NUTS

The novel pairing of sweet raisins with delicate pine nuts softens the bite of
the warmed dressing in this appealing salad.

2 POUNDS FRESH ESCAROLE, TRIMMED

2 TABLESPOONS OLIVE OIL

1 CLOVE GARLIC, MINCED

2 TABLESPOONS GOLDEN RAISINS

2 TABLESPOONS PINE NUTS, TOASTED

2 TEASPOONS RED WINE VINEGAR

SALT AND FRESHLY GROUND BLACK PEPPER TO TASTE

Thoroughly wash escarole in cold water; tear leaves coarsely.
Steam about 1-2 minutes, until just wilted; remove and set aside.

In a large skillet, heat olive oil and lightly sauté garlic. Add
escarole and remaining ingredients; stir to mix well. Warm
lightly. Serve on individual salad plates. Serves 6.

A Quick Lesson in *Pinoli*

Most famous for their flavorful addition to classic
pesto sauce, Italian pine nuts, or *pinoli*, perk up a variety
of sweet and savory dishes as well. They come from
the large cones of the stone pine tree native to Italy.
The process of extracting these meaty little nuts is
quite labor-intensive, which explains why they're so
prohibitively priced. But their delicate, nutty flavor is
worth the cost (and any recipe that suggests substituting
slivered almonds is not to be trusted). The trick is
to buy these little treasures from gourmet nut shops or
health food stores, where they're usually sold in bulk
for much less than you'll find them in supermarkets.
Pine nuts turn rancid fast—due to their high fat
content—but they can be stored safely in an airtight
container in the freezer for up to nine months or in the
refrigerator for up to three.

Pere cotte

POACHED PEARS

The ideal dessert: satisfying, sophisticated, and a cinch to make. For a pretty and fool-proof presentation, pick pears that are not overly ripe and have gracefully shaped stems.

6 BOSC PEARS

2 CUPS WATER

1 CUP SUGAR

2 CINNAMON STICKS

5 WHOLE CLOVES

ZEST OF 1 LEMON, CUT IN STRIPS

JUICE OF ½ LEMON

CINNAMON STICKS FOR GARNISH (OPTIONAL)

Peel pears, leaving stem intact. Using a small melon baller, remove stems and seeds from bottom of pears. In a saucepan that will accommodate pears upright, combine water, sugar, cinnamon sticks, cloves, lemon zest, and lemon juice. Bring to a boil. Add pears, cook over medium heat, maintaining a boil for 5 minutes. Remove from heat, allow pears to cool slowly; baste occasionally with poaching liquid. When completely cooled, chill pears. Arrange on individual dessert plates. Spoon liquid over pears; garnish with cinnamon sticks, if desired. Serves 6.

Cenetta davanti al caminetto

Fireside Dinner Party (Serves 6)

Serve this quintessential hearty fare when temperatures are approaching record lows, and watch your guests light (and warm) up. Call the party for an early start—perhaps just as the day's light is waning—as this is one meal that shouldn't be rushed. While preparation may entail the better part of an afternoon, none of these recipes requires last-minute tending. Which means that when the doorbell rings, everything will be ready and waiting.

CLAM AND BACON FOCACCIA

SHRIMP BISQUE

TUSCAN POT ROAST WITH WINTER VEGETABLES

TUSCAN BEAN AND BREAD SALAD

ALMOND CAKE

Focaccia alle vongole e pancetta
CLAM AND BACON FOCACCIA

This flavorful "surf-and-turf" variation on basic focaccia can be served warm or at
room temperature for equally enthusiastic reviews.

1 Baked Basic Focaccia, halved (see recipe, p. 33)

¼ cup torn fresh basil leaves

4 ounces fresh mozzarella cheese, drained and thinly sliced

1 can (6½ oz.) minced clams, drained

3 strips bacon, cooked and crumbled

Preheat oven to 425°F.

Prepare and bake focaccia as directed. Top with basil leaves, mozzarella slices, minced clams, and crumbled bacon. Bake 8-10 minutes or until cheese melts. Cut into squares to serve. Serves 6.

Crema di gamberi

SHRIMP BISQUE

Simmering the shrimp in the soup enhances the flavor of this zesty, warming, and wonderfully welcoming first course. For best results, adjust seasonings before serving.

1 MEDIUM ONION, FINELY CHOPPED

1 STALK CELERY, FINELY CHOPPED

1 RED BELL PEPPER, CHOPPED

2 CLOVES GARLIC, MINCED

2 TABLESPOONS BUTTER

3 CUPS FRESH TOMATO BASIL SAUCE (SEE RECIPE, P. 136)

1 CAN (13¾ OZ.) LOWER-SALT CHICKEN BROTH

HOT PEPPER SAUCE TO TASTE

12 OUNCES FRESH OR FROZEN SHRIMP, PEELED AND DEVEINED

1 CUP LIGHT CREAM

½ CUP HEAVY CREAM

FRESHLY GROUND BLACK PEPPER TO TASTE

FLAT-LEAF ITALIAN PARSLEY FOR GARNISH

In a medium stock pot, sauté onion, celery, red pepper, and garlic in butter until tender. Add sauce, broth, and Tabasco sauce; simmer over low heat about 15 minutes, stirring occasionally. Add shrimp; cook until shrimp just turns pink. Whisk in the light and heavy creams, season to taste, and heat just until soup is warmed through. Garnish with parsley. Serves 6-8.

Arrosto di manzo alla toscana con verdure d'inverno
TUSCAN POT ROAST WITH WINTER VEGETABLES

**Slivered garlic cloves are the secret tenderizer, colorful baby vegetables the
picturesque accompaniment, in this savory one-pot main course.**

2 POUNDS CHUCK, ROUND, OR RUMP ROAST OF BEEF

2 LARGE CLOVES GARLIC, CUT IN SLIVERS

1 TEASPOON EACH SALT AND FRESHLY GROUND BLACK PEPPER

¼ CUP OLIVE OIL

2 ONIONS, FINELY CHOPPED

3 CARROTS, FINELY CHOPPED

1 STALK CELERY, FINELY CHOPPED

⅔ CUP BEEF BROTH

2 CUPS MARINARA SAUCE WITH BURGUNDY WINE
(SEE RECIPE, P. 137)

½ CUP RED WINE

2 CUPS BABY CARROTS, PEELED

8 SMALL RED POTATOES, CUT IN HALF

1 CUP PEARL ONIONS OR SMALL WHITE ONIONS, PEELED

ROSEMARY SPRIGS FOR GARNISH

Make small slits in meat. Insert garlic slivers. Mix salt and pepper; sprinkle over meat. Heat olive oil in a Dutch oven; add meat and brown on all sides. Remove meat and set aside. Add chopped vegetables; cook about 10 minutes over low heat, stirring occasionally. Add beef broth and sauce; bring to a boil. Return meat to Dutch oven; cover and cook over low heat, stirring occasionally, about 1½ hours. Uncover pot, raise heat to medium, and add wine. Boil briskly about 2 minutes, until wine is nearly evaporated. Lower heat, cover, and cook over low heat about 30 minutes longer or until meat is very tender. Add baby carrots, potatoes, and onions. Simmer about 30 minutes or until vegetables are tender. Slice meat fairly thick; arrange on a serving platter surrounded by vegetables and ladle sauce over meat. Garnish with rosemary sprigs. Serves 6.

Insalata toscana di pane e fagioli

TUSCAN BEAN AND BREAD SALAD

Another example of the wonders Tuscan cooks work with days-old bread. Make more than you need of this tasty salad/side dish—it's even better the next day.

1 LOAF CRUSTY STALE BREAD, TORN IN BITE-SIZE PIECES

APPROXIMATELY ½ CUP WATER

1 SMALL ONION, CHOPPED

2 CLOVES GARLIC, MINCED

2 STALKS CELERY, THINLY SLICED

¼ CUP OIL-CURED BLACK OLIVES, PITTED

1 CAN (15½ OZ.) WHITE BEANS, DRAINED AND RINSED

¼ CUP EXTRA-VIRGIN OLIVE OIL

2 TABLESPOONS BALSAMIC VINEGAR

2 TABLESPOONS MINCED FRESH FLAT-LEAF ITALIAN PARSLEY

1 TEASPOON MINCED FRESH SAGE

1 TEASPOON FINELY GRATED ORANGE ZEST

SALT AND FRESHLY GROUND BLACK PEPPER TO TASTE

FRESH THYME SPRIGS FOR GARNISH

Sprinkle just enough water over bread to moisten without making it soggy; set aside. In a medium bowl, combine remaining ingredients; stir to mix well. Add bread cubes; toss to mix thoroughly and allow to set about 30 minutes. Transfer to serving bowl or platter. Garnish with thyme sprigs. Serves 6.

Torta di mandorle

ALMOND CAKE

Since no one can resist its almond aroma, this nice, light cake is the perfect ending to a substantial meal. Serve with fresh whipped cream for a dollop of decadence.

1½ CUPS FLOUR

½ CUP FINELY GROUND ALMONDS

1 TEASPOON BAKING POWDER

½ TEASPOON CINNAMON

¼ TEASPOON SALT

PINCH GROUND CLOVES

½ CUP UNSALTED BUTTER, SOFTENED

1 CUP SUGAR

2 LARGE EGGS

½ CUP FRESH ORANGE JUICE

1 TABLESPOON FINELY GRATED ORANGE ZEST

1 TEASPOON VANILLA EXTRACT

CONFECTIONERS' SUGAR

Preheat oven to 325° F.

Lightly grease and flour a 9-inch springform pan. In a large bowl, combine flour, almonds, baking powder, cinnamon, salt, and cloves; set aside. In a large bowl, beat the butter and sugar using an electric mixer at high speed until light. Beat in eggs. At low speed, gradually add orange juice, zest, and vanilla. Blend dry ingredients into egg mixture just until blended. Spread mixture into prepared pan. Bake 40-45 minutes until toothpick inserted in center comes out clean.

Cool in pan on a wire rack. Loosen sides of cake from pan using a knife. Unmold and transfer to a serving plate. Dust with sifted confectioners' sugar. Serves 10-12.

Colazione festosa

Festive Brunch Buffet (Serves 8 to 10)

Turn any day into a holiday with this simply spectacular brunch menu. It's as impressive as it is easy to prepare. If you've never tasted roasted garlic, you're in for a rare treat. The mixed antipasto salad is certain to receive rave reviews. The gnocchi dish is a nice celebratory touch. And be forewarned: you may want to make extra batches of these biscotti—they are, in a word, fabulous.

CROSTINI WITH ROASTED GARLIC

CLASSIC ANTIPASTO SALAD

GNOCCHI WITH CREAMY ROASTED RED PEPPER SAUCE

WARM LENTIL SALAD

ALMOND ANISE BISCOTTI

Crostini alle melanzane arrosto

CROSTINI WITH ROASTED GARLIC

**The simple trick to the most savory roasted garlic? Ferret out the whitest heads you can
find. Then make sure to roast just long enough, so the garlic spreads like butter.**

6 WHOLE GARLIC HEADS

OLIVE OIL

1½ CRUSTY BAGUETTES, SLICED ½-INCH THICK (ABOUT 10
SLICES)

Preheat oven to 375° F.

Cut off papery tips of stem end of garlic heads. Brush liberally with olive oil. Place in a garlic roaster or wrap garlic heads tightly in foil and place in a shallow baking dish. Bake about 1 hour or until garlic is very soft, but not browned.

Brush both sides of bread slices with olive oil and arrange on two baking sheets. Bake about 8 minutes or until lightly browned. Remove from oven. Spread roasted garlic on crostini. Best served warm. Makes 10 crostini.

Antipasto misto
CLASSIC ANTIPASTO SALAD

If time allows, prepare this everything-but-the-kitchen-sink salad days in advance; the flavors harmonize better the longer they're left to mingle.

Dressing:

1 CLOVE GARLIC, MINCED

2 TABLESPOONS BALSAMIC VINEGAR

½ TEASPOON DRIED BASIL

½ TEASPOON DRIED OREGANO

¼ TEASPOON ROSEMARY, CRUSHED

¼ TEASPOON CRUSHED RED PEPPER FLAKES

¼ CUP EXTRA-VIRGIN OLIVE OIL

Salad:

2 LARGE CARROTS, PEELED AND CUT DIAGONALLY INTO ¼-INCH SLICES

1 SMALL FENNEL BULB, CORED AND CUT INTO ¼-INCH SLICES

6 OUNCES HOMEMADE OR JARRED ROASTED RED OR YELLOW PEPPERS, CUT INTO STRIPS

1 JAR (9 OZ.) PEPPERONCINI, RINSED AND DRAINED WELL

6 OUNCES MIXED OIL-CURED OLIVES, PITTED

2 OUNCES SUN-DRIED TOMATOES, PACKED IN OIL, DRAINED AND CUT IN STRIPS

6 OUNCES MARINATED OR PLAIN BOCCONCINI (FRESH MOZZARELLA), QUARTERED

4 OUNCES PEPPERONI, QUARTERED AND SLICED

1 JAR (6 OZ.) MARINATED ARTICHOKE HEARTS, DRAINED

2 TABLESPOONS MINCED FRESH FLAT-LEAF ITALIAN PARSLEY

FRESH THYME FOR GARNISH

To prepare dressing, combine garlic, balsamic vinegar, basil, oregano, rosemary, and crushed red pepper flakes. Add olive oil slowly, whisking until mixture emulsifies.

Blanch carrots and fennel in boiling water for 3 to 4 minutes or until tender crisp; drain and place in a bowl of ice water to cool. When vegetables are cool, drain thoroughly. In a large bowl, combine all salad ingredients. Pour on dressing; toss to coat well. Refrigerate, covered, at least 4 hours or overnight. To serve, transfer salad to a platter; garnish with fresh thyme. Serves 8-10.

Gnocchi alla crema di peperoni rossi

GNOCCHI WITH CREAMY ROASTED RED PEPPER SAUCE

1 JAR (7 OZ.) ROASTED RED PEPPERS, DRAINED

½ CUP LOWER-SALT CHICKEN BROTH

¼ CUP SHERRY WINE

3 DROPS HOT PEPPER SAUCE

1 CUP HEAVY CREAM

3 TABLESPOONS FINELY CHOPPED FRESH BASIL

2 POUNDS FRESH OR FROZEN GNOCCHI, COOKED AND DRAINED

Purée roasted peppers in a food processor or blender; set aside. In a medium saucepan, combine purée, broth, sherry and Tabasco sauce; simmer over low heat 10-15 minutes. Stir in cream and set over medium heat. Simmer, stirring frequently, about 15 minutes or until slightly reduced. Remove from heat; stir in basil. Spoon sauce over hot gnocchi; toss to coat well. Serves 8-10.

Homemade Gnocchi in Five Steps

Italian for "dumplings," gnocchi (sometimes called *topini* in Tuscany, meaning "little mice") aren't all that difficult to make—and homemade are far more tasty than the store-bought varieties. Classic gnocchi are made from potatoes, but they can also be made from flour or cornmeal. To make a six-person serving of *gnocchi di patate*, or potato gnocchi, you need:

2 pounds baking potatoes, washed but not peeled

1 egg

½ teaspoon salt

2 cups flour

1: Steam potatoes until tender (about 30 minutes). While still hot, peel, place in a bowl and mash.

2: Mix in the egg and salt, and turn mixture onto a floured board.

3: Put up a pot of salted water (about 6 quarts) to boil. Knead the dough about 10 minutes, adding flour as necessary, until it forms a firm, smooth dough.

4: To form the dumplings, flour palms and board again. Break off small pieces of dough, and roll each into thin, cigar shapes with your palms. With a paring knife, cut each into inch-long pieces. Then gently press each one on the tines of a fork—for those characteristic ridges—pressing each in the center with your thumb. Set shaped gnocchi on floured napkins; this helps to absorb the moisture from the potatoes.

5: Drop gnocchi, several at a time, into boiling water and cook about three minutes or until they rise to the surface. Remove cooked gnocchi with a slotted spoon; drain well. Place on a platter and cover to keep warm while cooking remaining dumplings.

Insalata tiepida di lenticchie

WARM LENTIL SALAD

In Tuscany, lentils are said to bring prosperity if eaten during the last few days of the year. Consider this delectable side dish your lucky charm.

1 POUND DRY LENTILS

1 BAY LEAF

2 TEASPOONS FRESH THYME

6 CUPS LOWER-SALT CHICKEN BROTH, HOMEMADE OR CANNED

3 MEDIUM CARROTS, PEELED AND CHOPPED

1 WHOLE MEDIUM ONION, PEELED

½ CUP FRESH LEMON JUICE

½ CUP CHOPPED FRESH FLAT-LEAF ITALIAN PARSLEY

¼ CUP EXTRA-VIRGIN OLIVE OIL

¼ CUP SLICED SCALLIONS

SALT AND FRESHLY GROUND BLACK PEPPER TO TASTE

1 HEAD RADICCHIO, SEPARATED INTO LEAVES

In a large saucepan, combine lentils, bay leaf, thyme, carrots, onion, and broth; heat to boiling. Reduce heat to low; cover and simmer 20 to 25 minutes or until lentils are tender and broth is absorbed. Do not overcook. Remove and discard onion and bay leaf.

In a large bowl, combine lemon juice, parsley, olive oil, and scallions. Add lentils and toss. Season with salt and pepper. Line individual bowls with radicchio leaves and top with lentil salad. Serve warm or at room temperature. Serves 8-10.

Biscotti di mandorle all'anice

ALMOND ANISE BISCOTTI

**The tastiest way to eat these crunchy confections: dip twice in a glass of sweet
Vin Santo, Tuscany's favorite dessert wine.**

2½ CUPS FLOUR

2 TEASPOONS ANISE SEEDS

1½ TEASPOONS BAKING POWDER

½ TEASPOON SALT

½ CUP BUTTER, SOFTENED

1 CUP SUGAR

1 TABLESPOON GRATED ORANGE ZEST

2 EGGS

½ TEASPOON VANILLA EXTRACT

¼ TEASPOON ALMOND EXTRACT

1½ CUPS COARSELY CHOPPED ALMONDS

Preheat oven to 325° F.

In a medium bowl, combine flour, anise seeds, baking powder, and salt; set aside. Using an electric mixer, beat butter, sugar, and orange zest until light and fluffy. Beat in eggs, one at a time; add vanilla and almond extracts. Gradually beat in flour mixture. Stir in almonds. Divide dough in half. On an ungreased baking sheet, form into 2 flattened logs, each about 14 inches long × 3 inches wide. Place three inches apart on baking sheet. Bake 40 minutes or until light golden in color.

Reduce oven to 250° F. On a cutting board, cut logs crosswise on the diagonal into ¾-inch slices. Arrange biscotti cutside down on baking sheet. Bake 10 minutes on each side. Transfer biscotti onto rack to cool. Store in airtight container. Makes about 3 dozen.

Nella cucina toscana

IN THE TUSCAN KITCHEN

If working with the freshest ingredients is the essence of Tuscan cooking, stocking the kitchen with some basics—olive oil, vinegar, aromatic herbs, pasta, and beans—is the trade secret to creating its signature fare. Consider this chapter a resource for the cardinal elements to have on hand, as well as a glossary explaining how to best employ, and enjoy, the necessities of this simply wonderful cuisine. This chapter also includes recipes for the traditional Tuscan pasta sauces that are used as ingredients throughout this book.

Pastas and the Sauces that Suit Them

The word "pasta" means paste in Italian and refers to the dough made by combining semolina (durum wheat flour that is more coarsely ground than regular wheat flours) with water. Its origin is actually unknown; what is known, however, is that pasta, with its myriad appetizing flavors, has been central to the Tuscan table for centuries. And while this modest food group comes in literally hundreds of shapes, sizes, and thicknesses (more than 350, in fact), the following 25—which include both dried pasta and fresh (those that have eggs added to the dough)—are among the most popular and interesting. (Note: though every pasta is special, there's no sacrilege in substitution. For the most part, you may feel confident about swapping one similarly-sized pasta for another without fear of sabotaging a dish's integrity.)

• **Bucatini** (also known as *perciatelli*)—long, thick, hollow noodles that work best with zesty tomato-based sauces.

• **Cannelloni**—rectangles of fresh dough that are rolled into a large tube shape. A specialty of the Piedmont region, cannelloni are traditionally boiled, then stuffed with a meat or cheese filling and baked with a balsamella sauce (the Italian version of bechamel).

• **Capelli D'Angelo** (also called *capellini*)—"angel hair"; long, delicate noodles that serve up best with light sauces or broth.

• **Cappelletti**—"little hats"; tiny dumplings typically stuffed with a filling of chicken, pork, mortadella, ricotta, Parmesan, and nutmeg, served in a chicken broth.

• **Conchiglie**—"shells"; oblong shell shapes, pinched at each end. (Ridged styles are called *conchiglie rigate*.) They pair well with chunky meat sauces and vegetables.

• **Farfalle**—"butterflies"; bowtie-shaped pastas that are the perfect foil for light sauces studded with vegetables.

• **Fettuccine**—"little ribbons"; long, flat egg noodles, about ⅜-inch wide, that can stand up to the most substantial red or white sauces. Fettucine are the slightly narrower Roman version of *tagliatelle*—a commonly used pasta in Tuscany and a specialty of Bologna, where they're traditionally served with a meat-based sauce.

• **Fusilli**—short corkscrew shapes or long, curly strands (they can range from 1½ to 12 inches) that go well with thick creamy sauces, adorned with meat or vegetables. Unlike spaghetti, long fusilli do not work so well with simple oil-based sauces.

• **Lasagne**—flat, 2-inch broad strips of egg-noodle dough, often cut with a serrated pastry wheel for a ruffled edge. Its most celebrated version, lasagne verdi, is made with spinach-embellished dough and layered with Bolognese meat sauce and Parmesan and baked till bubbly.

• **Linguine**—"little tongues"; long, narrow noodles, about ⅛-inch wide—sometimes referred to as flat spaghetti—that work best with clinging sauces (think pesto or cream-based). A southern Italian pasta, linguine are rarely used in Tuscany; Tuscans favor spaghetti instead.

• **Lumache**—"snails"; resembling large conchiglie, they go well with the same kind of substantial sauces.

• **Orecchiette**—"little ears"; small, round, slightly concave shapes. A specialty of Apulia, these are traditionally served with a sauce of broccoli florets, olive oil, and anchovies, but work equally well with a variety of chunky white sauces.

• **Pappardelle**—the most Tuscan of pastas, broad egg noodles, about ½-inch wide, often cut with a serrated pastry wheel for a crimped edge; traditionally paired with game sauces, though any hearty meat sauce works well.

• **Pastine**—a variety of miniature pastas, including *annellini* ("little rings"), *ditalini* ("little thimbles"), *orzo* ("barley"), and *stelline* ("little stars"), that are most often served in clear-broth soups, topped with grated Parmesan.

- **Penne**—"quills"; short, hollow tubular shapes cut on the diagonal. (When ridged, they're called *penne rigate*.) These versatile noodles work as well with robust, chunky sauces as with the simplest tomato sauce.
- **Radiatori**—"radiators"; stubby spirals best suited to chunky sauces; also a good choice for cold pasta salads.
- **Ravioli**—the classic stuffed pasta, these square pillows of egg-noodle dough are filled with various stuffings of meat, cheese, or vegetables and best served with simple tomato sauce.
- **Rigatoni**—stubby, grooved tube shapes, larger and less delicate than penne, that stand up well to robust meat- or cream-based sauces.
- **Rotelle**—small, round noodles that resemble a wagon wheel; good with clingy vegetable sauces and sturdy enough for cold salads.
- **Rotini**—short, thin spirals that can handle the same types of sauces as radiatori and rotelle.
- **Spaghetti and spaghettini**—"strings"; the most well-known pasta, especially good with oil-based sauces that incorporate seafood or vegetables. (Spaghettini are the thinner version.) In Italy, spaghetti are never served with meatballs—that's an American invention.
- **Tagliatelle and tagliolini**—Tuscan favorites, long, flat strips, about ¼-inch wide (tagliolini are thinner); see fettuccine, above.
- **Tortellini**—"little twists"; small, ring-shaped egg-noodle dumplings. (*Tortelloni* are their larger counterparts.) A specialty of Bologna, traditionally stuffed with a meat or cheese filling and served in broth, but can stand up to cream-based and hearty tomato sauces.
- **Vermicelli**—"little worms"; long strands, thinner than spaghetti, that are best suited to simple oil-based or delicate sauces.
- **Ziti**—"bridegrooms"; smooth, straight-cut tubular shapes, narrower than rigatoni but can accommodate the same types of sauces; often served baked in a tomato sauce with cheese.

The Traditional Sauces of Tuscany

Many of the recipes in this book call for one or more of the traditional sauces of Tuscany to be used as ingredients. In the test kitchen, all of these recipes were prepared using Five Brothers sauces. Because of the special care with which they are prepared, Five Brothers sauces always taste fresh and delicious, and they are perfect for bringing the authentic flavor of the Tuscan kitchen to the traditional recipes that appear herein. Five Brothers savory red sauces are unique among jarred sauces—they are the only sauces that use hand-selected fresh tomatoes, picked, cooked, and packed the same day. (Most other pasta sauces are made from tomatoes that have been cooked and stored—for up to a year—before being made into sauce.) The Alfredo sauces are prepared with the same extraordinary care, using select aged Parmesan cheese, fresh butter, and sweet cream. Every ingredient in Five Brothers sauces is chosen because it meets the hightest standards—only the best is good enough for Five Brothers pasta sauce. The highest-quality imported olive oil, the most robust garlic, the freshest basil—each element complements the others. The end results of Five Brothers' passion for freshness and quality are sauces that taste like no others—full of flavor and redolent with the authenticity of *cucina toscana*.

For those devoted cooks who remain committed to making their sauce from scratch, we offer the following recipes, adapted from the Five Brothers' kitchens. Always use the freshest, ripest ingredients available; and remember, there is no substitute for hand-selected and fresh-picked summer tomatoes.

Fresh Tomato Basil Sauce

2 TABLESPOONS PURE IMPORTED OLIVE OIL

2 GARLIC CLOVES, CRUSHED

2 POUNDS VINE-RIPENED SUMMER PLUM TOMATOES, PEELED AND COARSELY CHOPPED

½ TEASPOON SALT

FRESHLY GROUND BLACK PEPPER TO TASTE

12 LEAVES FRESH BASIL, SHREDDED

In a large skillet, heat olive oil; add garlic and sauté over low heat for 1 minute; be careful not to brown. Raise heat to medium and add tomatoes, salt, and pepper. Bring to a simmer. Stirring frequently, cook, uncovered, about 15 minutes or until sauce is slightly thickened. Stir in basil for the last minute of cooking. Adjust seasonings as needed. Remove from heat. Makes about 2½ cups; enough for 1 pound pasta.

To peel fresh tomatoes: drop the tomatoes, a few at a time, into a large pot of boiling water for about 10 seconds. This will loosen their skins. Remove with a slotted spoon; peel, core, and halve. Using your fingers, scoop out seeds; allow juice to drain. The tomato pulp is now ready to chop.
Be sure to use only the freshest, vine-ripened tomatoes of summer. Summer is when tomatoes are at their peak, and only tomatoes that have ripened on the vine during the warm months of summer will be as juicy and flavorful as possible.

Grilled Summer Vegetable Sauce

¼ CUP PURE IMPORTED OLIVE OIL

1 SMALL YELLOW ONION, CHOPPED

1 STALK CELERY, DICED

1 MEDIUM RED BELL PEPPER, SEEDED AND DICED

1 MEDIUM ZUCCHINI, DICED

1¼ POUNDS VINE-RIPENED SUMMER PLUM TOMATOES, PEELED AND COARSELY CHOPPED

SALT AND FRESHLY GROUND BLACK PEPPER TO TASTE

1 TABLESPOON CHOPPED FRESH FLAT-LEAF ITALIAN PARSLEY

In a large skillet, heat olive oil; add onion and sauté over low heat 5 minutes. Stir in celery, pepper, and zucchini; raise heat to medium and cook for 10 minutes or until tender. Add tomatoes, salt, and pepper. Bring to a simmer. Stirring frequently, cook, uncovered, about 10 minutes or until sauce is slightly reduced. Add parsley; stir to heat through. Adjust seasonings as needed. Remove from heat. Makes about 2½ cups; enough for 1 pound of pasta.

Oven-Roasted Garlic and Onion Sauce

2 TABLESPOONS PURE IMPORTED OLIVE OIL

1 MEDIUM YELLOW ONION, CHOPPED

2 POUNDS VINE-RIPENED SUMMER PLUM TOMATOES, PEELED AND COARSELY CHOPPED

1 HEAD GARLIC, ROASTED (SEE RECIPE, P. 126)

2 TABLESPOONS CHOPPED FRESH FLAT-LEAF ITALIAN PARSLEY

SALT AND FRESHLY GROUND BLACK PEPPER TO TASTE

In a large skillet, heat olive oil; add onion and sauté over low heat 5 minutes. Raise heat to medium and add tomatoes, salt, and pepper. Stirring frequently, cook uncovered 10 minutes. Meanwhile, peel roasted garlic; in a small bowl, lightly mash with fork. Add garlic to sauce; cook, stirring, about 5 minutes longer or until sauce begins to thicken. Add parsley; stir to heat through. Adjust seasonings, as needed. Remove from heat. Makes about 2½ cups; enough for 1 pound pasta

Mushroom and Garlic Grill Sauce

¾ OUNCE DRIED PORCINI MUSHROOMS

¼ CUP OLIVE OIL

4 CLOVES GARLIC, PEELED AND FINELY CHOPPED

1 SMALL YELLOW ONION, PEELED AND COARSELY CHOPPED

2 POUNDS VINE-RIPENED SUMMER PLUM TOMATOES, PEELED AND COARSELY CHOPPED

SALT AND FRESHLY GROUND BLACK PEPPER TO TASTE

1 TABLESPOON CHOPPED FRESH FLAT-LEAF ITALIAN PARSLEY

In a small saucepan, combine porcini and ¾ cup water; heat to boiling. Remove from heat; let stand, covered, 15 minutes. Drain through a fine sieve or doubled cheesecloth; reserve ¼ cup liquid and set aside. Rinse mushrooms of any grit; coarsely chop.

In a large skillet, heat olive oil; add onion and garlic and sauté over low heat 5 minutes. Add mushrooms and mushroom liquid, raise heat to medium, and cook, stirring, for 3 minutes. Add tomatoes, salt, and pepper. Bring to a simmer. Stirring frequently, cook, uncovered, about 10 minutes or until sauce is slightly reduced. Add parsley; stir to heat through. Adjust seasonings, as needed. Remove from heat. Makes about 2 ½ cups; enough for 1 pound of pasta

Marinara with Burgundy Wine Sauce

3 TABLESPOONS PURE IMPORTED OLIVE OIL

1 MEDIUM YELLOW ONION, DICED

2 CLOVES GARLIC, CRUSHED

2 POUNDS VINE-RIPENED SUMMER PLUM TOMATOES, PEELED AND COARSELY CHOPPED

¼ CUP DRY BURGUNDY WINE

SALT AND FRESHLY GROUND BLACK PEPPER TO TASTE

1-2 TABLESPOONS CHOPPED FRESH OREGANO

In a large skillet, heat olive oil; add onion and sauté over low heat 5 minutes. Stir in garlic and saute 1 minute; do not brown. Raise heat to medium and add tomatoes, salt, and pepper. Bring to a simmer. Stirring frequently, cook, uncovered, 10 minutes. Add wine; raise heat and allow sauce to boil about 1 minute. Lower heat; cook, stirring, about 3 minutes longer or until sauce is slightly reduced. Add oregano; stir to heat through. Adjust seasonings, as needed. Remove from heat. Makes about 2½ cups; enough for 1 pound pasta

Creamy Alfredo Sauce

4 TABLESPOONS SWEET BUTTER

1½ CUPS FRESH SWEET CREAM

¼ CUP FRESHLY GRATED PARMESAN CHEESE

FRESHLY GROUND BLACK PEPPER TO TASTE

In a heavy saucepan, gently melt butter over low heat. Raise heat to medium-low and add cream; stir. Cook, covered, 5-10 minutes or until sauce has reduced and thickened. Whisk in Parmesan; heat through about 1 minute. Stir in pepper. Remove from heat and serve immediately. Makes about 2 cups; enough for 1 pound pasta.

A Few Notes on Sauce

In Tuscan cooking, sauce rules. Rather than spooning sauce over pasta, it becomes incorporated into the dish.

• After the pasta is cooked and drained, quickly add it to the steaming pot of sauce, and toss. This allows the noodles to be infused with the sauce's flavors.

• The rule of thumb for pairing pasta and sauce: the longer and finer the pasta, the lighter the sauce; likewise, the stubbier or broader the noodle, the chunkier and more substantial the sauce.

Olive Oil: Italy's Liquid Gold

Treated like fine wine in Tuscany, *olio d'oliva* is the most flavorful vegetable oil. It comes in several grades, each of which relates to the degree of acidity the oil contains. The classifications include:

• **Extra Virgin**—the finest quality, containing less than 1 percent acidity. This designation guarantees that the olives were hand picked and the oil extracted by the cold-press method (meaning, no heat or chemicals were used to speed the process)—which makes this the most expensive olive oil but also the most robust. Its color can range from greenish-golden to almost bright green; and typically, the deeper the color, the more intense the flavor. Not a cooking oil (the flavor breaks down when heated), extra virgin should be used only as a marinade, on salads, cold antipasti, topping off soups, and for a popular Tuscan treat: drizzled on slices of crusty peasant bread.

• **Fine Virgin**—containing not more than 2 percent acidity, making the flavor a hint more bitter. It's also paler in color. But it makes a reasonable stand-in for extra virgin (and it is not as pricey).

• **Semifine Virgin and Pure (also called Virgin)**—from later pressings of olives, processed under heat or with solvents. These grades contain less than 3.3 percent and not more than 4 percent acidity, respectively. Mildly flavorful, these are best suited to sauteing, low-heat cooking, or whenever your needs call for an unassertively flavored oil.

• **Light**—not to be confused with a caloric distinction (all oil contains the same amount of calories), this labeling refers to the oil's color, fragrance, and flavor. Produced using a newer filtration process that gives it a higher smoke point than other olive oils, light is the perfect choice for frying and roasting, as well as for baking.

Pleasantly Pungent Vinegars

Wine vinegars are the standard-bearers in Tuscan cuisine. Red takes precedence over white—unless a particular recipe is cream-based, in which case Tuscan cooks will opt for a white-wine vinegar, so as not to discolor the dish. The fragrant *aceto balsamico*, or balsamic vinegar, is also popular among the trendier cooks in Tuscany. This exquisite vinegar from Modena, in northern Italy's Emilia-Romagna region, is made from the cooked and concentrated must of white Trebbiano grapes. (And since the grapes are never left to ferment, it's technically not a wine vinegar.) It gets its warm brown color and sweetly sour taste from an aging process that requires a minimum of 10 years and a succession of various wooden barrels. Use balsamic vinegar to make a wonderful vinaigrette (one part vinegar to three parts oil), or splash it in sauces and marinades, on vegetables, even cooked fruit.

All vinegars should be stored airtight in a cool, dark place. Once opened, they will keep for about six months.

Flavorful Herbs

In Tuscan cooking, fresh herbs are most often added to a dish as a final touch—for the most aromatic, lasting impression. And while fresh is almost always the operative word, exceptions can be made for bay leaves, marjoram, and oregano, whose dried forms are sufficiently flavorful, and for which a little goes a long way (though after six months, they quickly lose their pungency). Here, a quick rundown of the most characteristically Tuscan herbs:

• **Basil** (*basilico*)—the most glamorous of cooking herbs, with a delightful aroma and flavor. Use fresh only. For maximum shelf life (up to five days), trim off roots and store, stems down, in a glass of water in the refrigerator, with a plastic bag over the leaves; change water every other day.

• **Bay leaves** (*alloro*)—extremely pungent, with a bit of a sour bite (overuse can make a dish taste bitter). Unless a recipe notes otherwise, always remove before serving, and never ingest. For maximum shelf life (up to six months), keep dried bay leaves in an airtight jar, and store in a cool, dark place.

• **Marjoram** (*maggiorana*)—closely related to oregano but milder and sweeter in flavor. Available fresh, but more often used dried. For maximum shelf life, follow storage suggestion for bay leaves.

• **Mint** (*menta*)—aromatic and flavorful, with a refreshingly sweet, pepperminty taste. Use fresh only. For maximum shelf life (up to seven days), follow storage suggestion for basil.

• **Oregano** (*origano*)—one of the definitive flavors of Italian cooking, with a pungent, almost spicy taste. Use fresh or dried.

For maximum shelf life, follow storage suggestion for bay leaves.

• **Parsley** (*prezzemolo*)—an indispensable Italian herb, flat-leaf, or Italian, parsley has a clean, fresh flavor that enhances the taste of other herbs. Use fresh only. For maximum shelf life (up to 10 days), rinse, shake off excess moisture and wrap in a paper towel; place in a plastic bag and refrigerate.

• **Rosemary** (*rosmarino*, or *ramerino* in Tuscan vernacular)—among the most aromatic herbs, these sprigs of silver-green, small needle-shaped leaves have a scent and flavor that hint of both lemon and pine. Use fresh only. For maximum shelf life (up to 10 days), wrap in a damp paper towel and place in a plastic bag and refrigerate. Do not rinse before refrigerating. Freezing fresh rosemary is an option—it will keep for up to two months—though its flavor may dissipate.

• **Sage** (*salvia*)—this pungent herb's leaves have a slightly bitter mint taste and aroma. Use fresh only—and add at the end of the cooking process. For maximum shelf life (up to four days), follow storage suggestion for rosemary.

Beans: Trademarks of Tuscan Cooking

Beans are so prevalent in Tuscan dishes that the people of Tuscany have been lovingly nicknamed *mangiafagioli*, "bean eaters." The cuisine's most frequently used beans—available dried, canned, and fresh—include:

• **Borlotti beans**—cream-colored oval beans with red streaks that have a nutlike flavor; also known as cranberry beans.

• **Cannellini beans**—white, thin-skinned kidney-shaped beans with a smooth flavor; often called Tuscan beans.

• **Chickpeas** (*ceci*)—buff-colored round beans with a firm texture and mildly nutlike taste; also called garbanzo beans.

• **Fava beans** (*fave*)—tan, rather flat oval-shaped beans with a buttery texture and slightly nutty flavor; also known as broad beans. A Tuscan favorite, they are delicious pureed, marinated in oil and herbs, or served raw with salt, to be shelled and eaten like peanuts.

• **Lentils** (*lenticchie*)—tiny grayish-brown button-shaped beans with a creamy yellow interior and slightly crunchy texture and mild taste.

Olives: An Italian Fruit

There are myriad varieties to choose from. The only rule: go for a selection of fresh, imported olives that have been cured in brine or vinegar, dry-cured in salt, and/or packed in oil. Canned olives (more of an American invention) have no charm and even less taste. Most of the imports are unpitted, however, and need to be pitted for use in prepared dishes.

• The trick to pitting: line up several olives at a time on a cutting board. Lay the broad end of the flat side of the blade of a large chef's knife on top of the olives, and hit the blade hard with the heel of your hand to crack the flesh. Once the olive is opened, simply slip out the pit with your fingers.

- Store fresh olives in their own liquid—in a nonmetal container—in the refrigerator; they will keep for several weeks.

Arborio Rice

Most Tuscans would say that these hard-grain, high-starch, Italian-grown kernels exist solely for making risotto. That's because the ample starch quotient in this rice allows it to cook up into a creamy consistency, while allowing each grain to remain distinct and relatively firm. Look for arborio rice in Italian markets, gourmet shops, and select grocery stores. It's worth the search if you care at all about your risotto dishes. And if you've ever tried substituting regular rice in recipes calling for arborio, you're obviously a believer already.

Bread: The Staff of Tuscan Life

Pane toscano, or Tuscan bread—a light, crusty round loaf that also goes by the name of peasant bread—is a bona fide staple of this regional cuisine. One of the bread's more distinguishing characteristics is that it contains no salt because centuries ago, the high tax levied on salt made the commodity too rich for peasant blood. In time, though, such poverty-borne necessity turned into an ingenious culinary component—as it became clear that the absence of salt made this bread the perfect accompaniment to every meal. With its pleasingly neutral taste, it never overpowers or clashes with the flavor of other foods. Tuscan fare is also known for several other interesting breads, including focaccia—a large, flat, rectangular or round bread, cooked in a heavily oiled baking tin (see page 33)—and *schiacciata*—another type of flat bread, thinner and coarser than focaccia. And in the kitchens of Tuscany, no amount of bread, no matter how stale, is ever discarded—an obvious throwback to poorer times—which is why you'll find bread

turning up as a key, if uncommon, ingredient in the region's signature soups, stews, and salads. Two beautiful results of such pragmatism are these popular Tuscan antipasti:
- **Crostini**—small, fairly thin rounds of toasted bread (usually from baguette), brushed with extra-virgin olive oil and topped with a range of savory garnishes, from a simple olive or anchovy paste to goat cheese to (a true Tuscan delicacy) minced sauteed chicken livers. Think of these as Italy's answer to France's canapes.
- **Bruschetta**—thick slices of peasant bread; grilled, then rubbed with whole garlic cloves, drizzled with extra-virgin olive oil and seasoned with salt and pepper. The original garlic bread, it can be eaten as is, or topped with chopped ripe tomatoes, fresh basil, mozzarella, and other variations on a theme.

The Cheeses of Italy

Though Tuscany is not known for its cheese production—with the exception of Pecorino Toscano—Tuscans, like the rest of their fellow countrymen, know how to enjoy a host of cheeses. The following is only a partial list of the many delectable Italian cheeses to try:
- **Asiago**—semifirm with a rich nutty flavor, made from whole or part-skim cow's milk. Young, it's a table cheese; aged more than a year, it takes on a sharper taste and becomes hard enough to grate.
- **Bel Paese**—mild, semisoft with a buttery flavor, made from whole cow's milk; means "beautiful country."
- **Fontina**—creamy, semifirm with a mildly nutty flavor, from the Val d'Aosta region in northwest Italy; it both slices easily and melts smoothly, making it a dual table and cooking cheese.
- **Gorgonzola**—made from whole cow's milk, with a creamy texture and pungent flavor. Named after a village in Lombardy, it's considered one of the top three bleu cheeses in

the world. Gorgonzola *dolce* (also called *dolcelatte*) is a younger, softer, more mild version.

• **Mascarpone**—an ultrarich, double- to triple-cream soft dessert cheese made from whole cow's milk, with a delicate flavor and a consistency of softly whipped butter; the star of the classic dessert, tiramisu.

• **Mozzarella**—the most flavorful, and best, is mozzarella *di bufala*, made fresh from water-buffalo's milk. For cooking and shredding, choose a firmer whole cow's-milk mozzarella. (Stick with fresh mozzarella only; the packaged blocks sold in supermarkets don't do the name justice.)

• **Parmigiano-Reggiano**—the royalty of Italian cheeses; firm with a granular texture and savory salty taste, the result of years of aging; used primarily for grating and best when freshly grated.

• **Pecorino Romano**—sharp, salty aged cheese made from sheep's milk; typically used for grating over pasta dishes. Pecorino Toscano, from the province of Siena, has a slightly richer, more pungent flavor.

• **Provolone**—hard and sliceable; when young, has a delicate, buttery taste and when aged, becomes sharper and smokier.

• **Ricotta**—rich, moist with a delicate, almost sweet taste; made fresh from the whey drained off while making mozzarella or provolone. (In the U.S., ricotta is usually made from a mix of whey and whole or skim milk.)

• **Taleggio**—rich, semisoft with a piquant flavor that grows stronger and runnier with age; both a table and cooking cheese.

Pairing Cheese and Fruit

In cucina toscana, dessert is often as simple as a combination of cheeses and fruits. Fruit is a refreshing accompaniment to rich cheeses, and the right unions mutually enhance their select flavors. Here, some perfect pairings to try:

• Bel Paese with red grapes, apples, and pears
• Fontina with fresh figs and cherries
• Gorgonzola with pears and apples
• Gorgonzola dolce with peaches
• Mascarpone with strawberries, raspberries, blackberries, and peaches
• Mozzarella with melons
• Parmigiano-Reggiano with pears
• Taleggio with plums

Best Ways to Store Cheese

Soft, semisoft and semifirm cheeses should be wrapped individually, first in foil, then in plastic wrap, and refrigerated in the dairy compartment or vegetable crisper.

• Hard cheeses should be wrapped in a damp cloth to prevent dry out and refrigerated the same way.
• Store fresh mozzarella in the brine it's preserved in. Because it's fresh and ripens rapidly, it keeps for only a few days.
• Soft cheeses can be safely stored in the freezer to preserve their flavor—to thaw, unwrap and allow to return to room temperature; hard cheeses tend to crumble when frozen.
• All cheeses, except fresh, should be served at room temperature.

PHOTOGRAPHY CREDITS

scenic photography: ©Jeff Weir and ©Jeff Brall
food photography: ©Jeff Weir
photography on p. 36: ©Billy Arce